LIFE:
THE SECRET INSTRUCTION MANUAL

LIFE: THE SECRET INSTRUCTION MANUAL
First published by Alexander Coppen 2024 in the United States Of America.

Copyright © 2024 by Alexander Coppen

Citation(s):

Coppen, A. (2024). Life: The secret instruction manual. ISBN 979-8-99-165530-9.
Coppen, Alexander. Life: The Secret Instruction Manual. 2024. ISBN 979-8-99-165530-9.

The author may be contacted via email at ac@devilslane.com for enquiries or corrections. If you are an ordained minster involved in Christian apologetics for an established church, you may request an electronic copy of this book for free.

FIRST EDITION

ISBN: 979-8-99-165530-9 (print)
ISBN: 979-8-99-165531-6 (electronic)

Library of Congress Control Number: 2024921731

For Zair, Ollie, James.
So you can have the missing instruction manual I didn't. Or perhaps the wisdom I simply refused to pay attention to, when I could have.

Proverbs are always platitudes until you have personally experienced the truth of them.

—Aldous Huxley

Contents

X   Filling The Gaps

Preface

Nobody knows exactly when the Book of Proverbs was written. Estimates range from the tenth to the fourth century BC[1][2][3]. King Solomon, the second child of King David and Bathsheba, was regarded as the wealthiest and wisest man in the world through his forty year reign during 970–931 BC, and authored over three thousand "parallel" comparison sayings (aka "proverbs") during his lifetime[4][5]. It is believed he had seven hundred wives, three hundred concubines, two daughters (*Taphath, Basmath*), and a son (*Basmath*). Israel gained its highest splendour and wealth during his tenure[6].

Solomon was particularly esteemed across ancient kingdoms for his extraordinary wisdom and insight. His infamous judgment between two women laying claim to the same infant (1 Kings 3:16–28) is given as a profound illustration of his

[1] Dell, K. J. (2006). *The Book of Proverbs in Social and Theological Context*. Cambridge University Press.

[2] Fox, M. V. (2009). *Proverbs 1-9: A new translation with introduction and commentary*. Yale University Press.

[3] McKane, W. (1970). *Proverbs: A new approach*. SCM Press.

[4] Longman III, T. (2002). *How to Read Proverbs*. InterVarsity Press.

[5] Crenshaw, J. L. (2010). *Old Testament wisdom: An introduction* (3rd ed.). Westminster John Knox Press.

[6] Keil, C. F., & Delitzsch, F. (1996). *Commentary on the Old Testament (Vol. 3)*. Hendrickson Publishers.

discernment and prudence.

The Book of Proverbs has three other identified authors than Solomon. Firstly "The Wise" (22:17-24:22, 24:23-34); secondly, "Agur son of Jakeh" (30:1-33); and lastly, "King Lemuel" (31:1-9)[7]. It is formed of thirty-one chapters, or "collections", typically containing around thirty individual observations. In total, the book has nine hundred and fifteen verses.

It is written to a young man, whose identity or age is not known. He is only referred to as "my son". However, it most likely the audience was generalised to many or most young men[8].

Its purpose was for this young man, or these young men, to know wisdom and instruction (1:2); receive teaching in wise dealing, righteousness, justice and equity (1:3); help the simple gain prudence and the youth gain knowledge and discretion (1:4); increase learning and to acquire skill in understanding (1:5); understand proverbs, parables, wise sayings, and riddles (1:6); and to learn the fear of the Lord (1:7).

As it is a book written for young men, wisdom is personified as what young men crave and chase: a beautiful woman. Conversely, temptation is also personified as a young woman[9]. Yet it contains possibly the most beautiful description of womanhood in antiquity.

Proverbs are simple statements anyone can understand.

---

[7] Murphy, R. E. (1998). *Proverbs (Vol. 22)*. Thomas Nelson.

[8] Fox, M. V. (2000). *Proverbs 1-9: A New Translation with Introduction and Commentary*. Yale University Press.

[9] Clifford, R. J. (1999). *Proverbs: A Commentary*. Westminster John Knox Press.

They contrast and compare two things, such as different types of people or comparable situations. Each verse compresses a book's worth of wisdom into one single sentence a child can grasp.

The wisdom of this book is endless, deep, and free to all. Thousands of years of emergent knowledge, available to anyone, anywhere, at any time, without any charge whatsoever. What it teaches is timeless, priceless, and profound; yet simple, practical, and easily applicable to ordinary life. There is no-one whose life will not improve from merely reading it.

Why should you care what an old book says?

Times change, but human nature doesn't. What is written in the Book of Proverbs is eternal; the same problems and weaknesses occur today as they did three thousand years ago. Ours may not be an age of kings and slaves, but it is one of CEOs and wage slaves. Adultery may not get the death sentence, but people are still adulterous.

It might seem trite, but the Book of Proverbs was one of the first major attempts by humanity to write wisdom down and pass it along an inherited tradition. A way to teach and study wisdom rather than learn it by painful, repetitive experience. It lives on today, for you to immerse yourself within and become prudent. It is a gift to all generations which has borne fruit for millennia.

Acknowledgments

You will notice repetition in many paragraphs throughout this book, as you would in the Book of Proverbs. It is *deliberate*.

We learn by repetition. So much of our ordinary lives involves knowledge and behaviour which cross over, as does wisdom. As you read these chapters, you will begin to recognise blocks you have seen before; as you should recognise wisdom which is useful elsewhere in different situations.

You'll also notice the language and writing style is simple. Plain, in fact. As is noted in 10:19, the idea of obscuring our words to sound clever - or "multiplying" them - is dishonest in nature. Proverbs are basic, pithy observations which are preventative in their design, and meant to be understood by the simple so they instruct and edify.

This book is for men without fathers. Or fathers who were so distant, foolish, or indifferent they didn't care enough to impart the importance of wisdom, or bestow it like masculinity itself.

In Psalm 27, David says:

> *"Although my father and my mother have forsaken me, the LORD will take me in."*

And in Psalm 68, he explains why:

A father to the fatherless, a defender of widows, is God in his holy dwelling. God sets the lonely in families, he leads out the prisoners with singing; but the rebellious live in a sun-scorched land.

I

What Life Is

We all start the same way, and there are a limited number of paths ahead of us. Who you are, and the nature of your life, is determined by which you choose. Or if you choose at all.

Meet Lady Wisdom

Out in the open she calls aloud, she *raises her voice* in the public square; on top of the wall she *cries out*, at the city gate she makes her speech. At the highest point along the way, where the paths meet, she takes her stand; beside the gate leading into the city, at the entrance, she *cries aloud*.

She has built her house; she has set up its seven pillars. She has prepared her meat and mixed her wine; she has also set her table. She has sent out her servants, and she calls from the highest point of the city,

> *Let all who are simple come to my house!*

To those who have no sense she says,

> *Come, eat my food and drink the wine I have mixed. Leave your simple ways and you will live; walk in the way of insight.*

Listen, for I have trustworthy things to say; I open my lips to speak what is right. My mouth speaks what is true, for my lips hate evil. All the words of my mouth are just; none of them is crooked or perverse. To the discerning all of them are right;

they are upright to those who have found knowledge. Choose my instruction instead of silver, knowledge rather than choice gold, for wisdom is more precious than rubies, and nothing you desire can compare with me.

I, wisdom, dwell together with prudence; I possess knowledge and discretion. To fear the Lord is to hate evil; I hate pride and arrogance, evil behaviour and perverse speech. Counsel and sound judgment are mine; I have insight, I have power.

By me kings reign and rulers issue decrees that are just; by me princes govern, and nobles—all who rule on earth. I love those who love me, and those who seek me find me. With me are riches and honor, enduring wealth and prosperity. My fruit is better than fine gold; what I yield surpasses choice silver. I walk in the way of righteousness, along the paths of justice, bestowing a rich inheritance on those who love me and making their treasuries full.

The Lord brought me forth as the first of his works, before his deeds of old; I was formed long ages ago, at the very beginning, when the world came to be When there were no watery depths, I was given birth, when there were no springs overflowing with water; before the mountains were settled in place, before the hills, I was given birth, before he made the world or its fields or any of the dust of the earth.

I was there when he set the heavens in place, when he marked out the horizon on the face of the deep, when he established the clouds above and fixed securely the fountains of the deep when he gave the sea its boundary so the waters would not overstep his command, and when he marked out the foundations of the earth.

Then I was constantly at his side. I was filled with delight day after day, rejoicing always in his presence, rejoicing in his whole world and delighting in mankind.

Now then, my children, listen to me; blessed are those who keep my ways. Listen to my instruction and be wise; do not disregard it. Blessed are those who listen to me, watching daily at my doors, waiting at my doorway. For those who find me find life and receive favour from the Lord. But those who fail to find me harm themselves; all who hate me love death.

Make Your Choice

All children are born foolish (22:15). You have a choice. To spend your life trying to live well and make good decisions (4:26-27, 16:1, 20:11), or to not bother and end up in disaster due to your own lack of sense (1:32-33). God gave you senses to perceive the world around you (20:12), and your life reflects the contents of your heart as water reflects your face (27:19).

People have sets of ways they walk in, and life is a choice between these (2:9-10, 2:20, 20:24). You may see an ordinary road in front of you which seems like it seems right, but what you can't see is it leads to death (14:12, 16:25, 21:2, 21:16).

The right road ahead is straight and well-established, but all the wrong ways are crooked and go nowhere (2:13, 4:11). If you make that wise choice, you should look straight ahead and not go left or right (4:25-26), and put aside all your own notions and exclusively trust God to guide you down it (3:5-6, 16:21, 20:24, 23:19) to prosperity (28:25). Correction and instruction will be like a lamp providing light (6:23). You make the plans, and God carries you along the route He has planned for His own purpose (16:9, 19:21, 20:24).

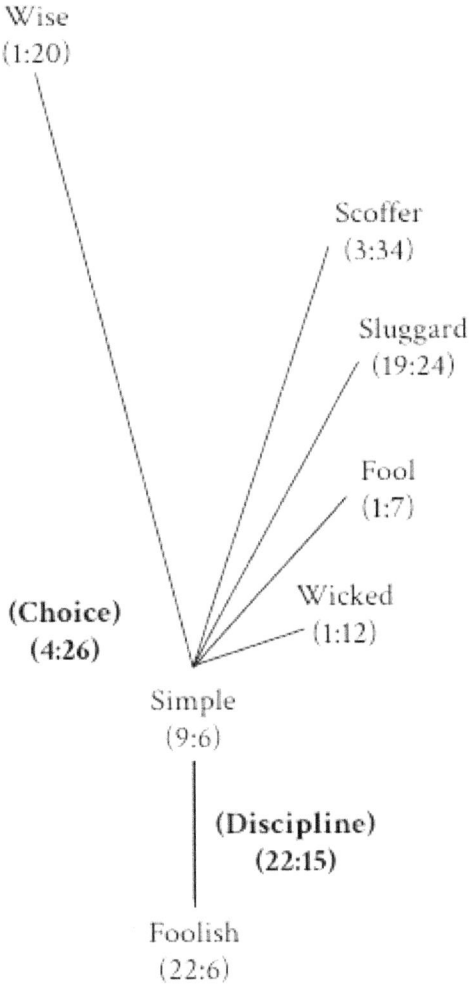

Wise
(1:20)

Scoffer
(3:34)

Sluggard
(19:24)

Fool
(1:7)

Wicked
(1:12)

(Choice)
(4:26)

Simple
(9:6)

(Discipline)
(22:15)

Foolish
(22:6)

Logic + Reason = Fear Of God

Belief in God is often a process rather than an event, and for some, often takes a lifetime. Different religious and philosophical can be categorised as viewpoints based on their characteristics related to the nature and attributes of divinity.

Most people start without knowledge ("a-gnosis") or care for the spiritual realm, immersed in material concerns. They are undecided, or believe the existence of a God cannot be known or proven.

If they come to a decision, their thinking tends to be a binary choice of disbelief in any divine entity ("a-theism"), or the possibility of its existence. The natural question then emerges of whether there is a single entity ("mono-theism") or more than one ("poly-theism").

Panentheism posits a god is both transcendent and immanent, existing within and beyond the universe; Pantheism equates a god with the universe itself, with no distinction between the creator and the creation. Theism distinguishes between a god who intervenes in the world, and one who does not.

indecision ———————— decision
(agnosticism)

no divine   divine
(atheism)

many gods   one God
(polytheism)

finite   infinite

personal   impersonal   personal   impersonal
(finite   (panentheism)   (pantheism)
Godism)

miracles   no miracles
(theism)   (deism)

triune   unipersonal
(Christian theism)   (unitarianism)

Alternatively, we can look at religious belief as a classification of metaphysical philosophy (how we think about the physical world we live in). Belief systems can be divided by whether they accept a structured and understandable reality, i.e. whether it has an intelligible purpose, or not.

When there is no understandable reality. Existence is there for its own sake. Individuals are free and responsible for determining their own development through acts of the will. Or life itself is meaningless.

The question then becomes the source of the coherence we observe that reality possesses. Everything arises from natural properties and causes which can be scientifically uncovered and supernatural or spiritual explanations are excluded, or there is an existence beyond the observable natural world, where supernatural forces and beings (e.g., gods, spirits) do exist.

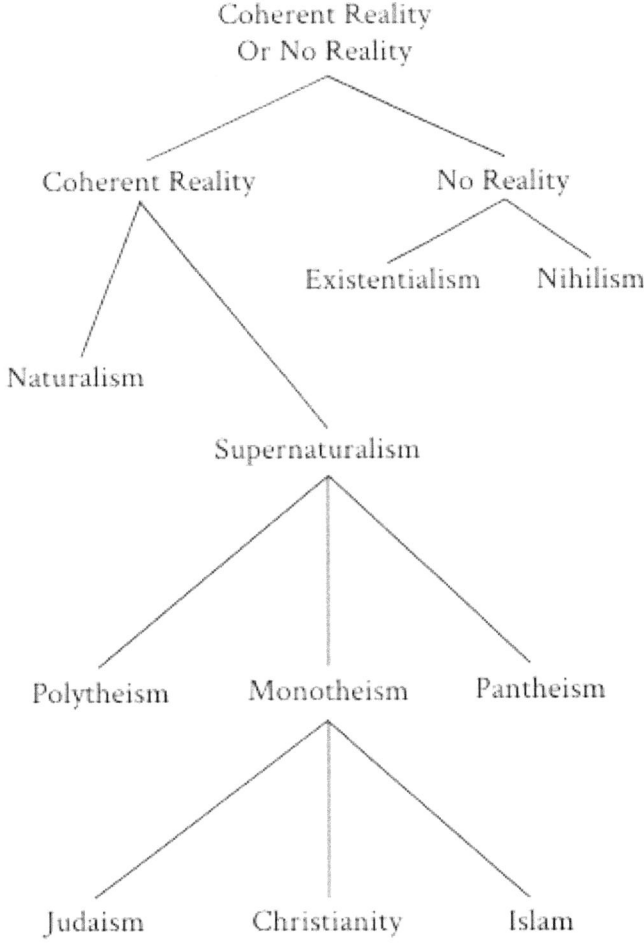

Who God Is

In a world of cause and effect, God is the Uncaused First Cause. He is the omnipresent, omniscient, omnipotent super-intelligence who created the 3D spacetime manifold of matter and energy everything exists within.

"El" is a word found frequently in the Bible for "god"; it forms terms such as *Eloah* (deity, singular) and *Elohim* ("gods", plural). God has many titles which describe Him, but He also has personhood and a *name*. In Exodus 3:13-15, Moses asks God what it is. God replies His name is *YHWH* (הוהי). Ancient Hebrew does not use vowels, but it translates in English to "I AM", or "Yahweh", which describes His timeless nature. In Judaism, the Divine Name is replaced by *HaShem* ("the Name", משה) or *Adonai* ("Lord", משה).

He is not an abstract *thing*. He is a *person*. His name is "I AM".

He made the universe and skies (3:19, 8:27), planet Earth (3:19, 8:26, 8:29), the oceans and continents (3:20), and the clouds (3:20, 8:28). He settled the mountains and hills in place (8:25), marked out the horizon (8:27), and gave the sea its boundary (8:29). He gave us eyes and ears so we could sense and perceive the world around us (20:12), and controls the lifespan and history of all things from beginning to end; even evil people and their deeds (16:4, 16:9).

He is to be feared (1:7, 2:5), and is the source of wisdom itself (2:6, 8:22). It's his prerogative and glory to conceal things (25:2). Nothing is beyond Him. He can see Heaven and Hell (15:9).

He is the Maker of everyone, rich or poor (22:2). He can see everything we do (5:21, 15:3, 20:27), and the contents of every person's heart (15:9. 20:27, 24:12). He weighs and measures our hearts (21:2, 24:12), and tests them (17:3, 20:27, 21:2, 24:12). He examines our internal motives (16:2, 20:27, 21:2, 24:12), and the subsequent choices we make (5:21, 20:27).

He delights in people who are trustworthy (12:22) and try to live a blameless life (11:20). He shows favour to people who are humble (3:34) or oppressed (3:34). The prayers of good people please him (15:8) and he hears them (15:29). He loves honest business with accurate measures (11:1, 16:11, 20:10), because He is completely trustworthy in all things (3:5-6).

He disciplines those He loves (3:12), and intervenes to prevent His children from being snared in traps (3:26). He takes in those who try to do the right thing and blesses their homes (3:32-33). He saves good people from hunger (10:3), acting as a shield and refuge to His children (30:5).

He hates greed and haughty eyes (6:17); lying and people who lie (6:17, 6:19, 8:13, 12:22); perverse people (3:32, 11:20); evil people (8:13); people who run to do evil (6:18); the condemnation of the innocent (17:15); the killing of the innocent (6:17); false testimony (6:18); scheming (6:18); people who stir up trouble in communities (6:19); pride (8:13, 16:5); arrogance (8:13); vile speech (8:13); cheating with dishonest scales (11:1, 20:10, 20:23); acquittal of the guilty (17:15); gifts and religious posturing from evil people (15:8, 21:27), particularly when it's for their own advancement (21:27). People who despise God are devious (14:2).

He oppresses the evil (10:3), and distances himself from them (15:29). He mocks arrogant cynics (3:33), and He acts against proud people. He punishes them by tearing down the source of their pride: what they've built for themselves (15:25, 16:5)

His Word, and every word He speaks, is flawless (30:5). Don't try to augment it or improve it, because He'll rebuke and shame you for it (30:6). He always has the final say, even in what appears random like a roll of the dice (16:33, 21:31). No human-devised course of action can thwart Him or succeed against Him (21:30).

What Wisdom Is

Wisdom comes from God; He is the ultimate source of it (2:6, 8:22-31) and His name alone is a powerful fortified tower (18:10). You should think of wisdom as sweet honey (24:14) more profitable than silver (3:14, 4:11, 8:19, 16:16), a better investment than gold (3:14, 8:10, 8:19, 16:16), more precious than rubies (3:15, 8:11), and search for it like a hidden treasure (2:4) which is unable to compare to than anything you could think of desiring (3:15, 4:7, 8:11). God verbalises it as speech from his mouth (2:6) and keeps meticulous watch over it (22:12).

The benefits of wisdom are you live in safety, feel at ease, and don't need to worry about being harmed (1:33, 3:23). It protects and guards you (2:11, 4:6, 6:22, 9:12) to give you hope and peace (3:2, 23:18), brings you an inheritance of honour (3:35, 4:8), and is spiritually pleasant (2:10, 3:17). It will protect your physical body (3:8, 3:22, 4:22), help you sleep well at night without anxiety or nightmares (3:24), extend your life expectancy (4:10,7:2, 9:11,10:27), and make you prosperous (3:2, 19:8). You won't have to fear sudden disaster or ruin (3:25, 4:12, 23:18).

All wisdom starts with understanding who God is and how powerful He is. Understanding his position as the Creator and author of all life, compared to yours as a simple primate who cannot change their own nature by themselves. The right response is humility: fear, respect, and reverence. (1:7, 9:10, 14:16, 22:4, 24:21). It means to hate evil, pride, arrogance, and vile speech (8:13). Just fearing Him means you are on the right track (14:2, 15:33, 16:6, 28:14) and behind the walls of a powerful fortress which will protect your family and children (14:26), turn you away from lethal traps (14:27, 19:23, 29:25), and be a fountain of life (14:27, 16:22, 19:23).

Wisdom was how God brought Creation into being (3:19-20). It is how kings reign, princes govern, nobles rule, and legislators issue decrees and laws (8:15-16). One wise person can walk through the doors of the largest fortress and pull its walls down in front of its strongest defenders (21:22).

The difference between wisdom and foolishness is the ability to accept instruction and correction. Listen to advice and respect those who are wiser than you. If you do, you will end up being one of them (19:20).

You can learn it. (1:23, 22:17-19, 23:12) It means to think about the right way to live (14:8) and the right steps to take (14:15). The first steps to start with are :

1. consistently fearing God (1:7, 14:16, 22:4, 23:17);
2. listening to your parents' teaching (1:8), and
3. avoiding any involvement with evil people (1:10-19, 14:16).

Afterwards, it's a process of never letting it out of your sight (3:21, 4:21), holding fast to it as a source of life (3:18, 4:13) and storing up commands (2:1, 4:4, 7:1, 10:8, 19:16) so wisdom lives in your heart (2:10) and you are blessed (3:18, 10:6, 29:18).

If you do, your name will be used in blessings (10:7) and you will love life (19:8).

It will start to come easily to you (14:6) as God tests and refines your heart (17:3) to produce patience (19:11). It is an endeavour which will crown you as royalty from the maturity and judgment you earn (14:18) and earn you a good reputation (16:21).

And you can teach it to others to guide them away from a ruinous life of disaster and foolishness (13:14). A person who loves wisdom always craves more wisdom (15:14) because their heart and ears crave it (18:15). They provide fantastic advice and instruction (16:23).

When people don't have Godly counsel or revealed wisdom to instruct them, they stop trying to behave virtuously and indulge hedonistically in undisciplined sin (29:18).

The consequences of not making any effort to become wise are severe: disaster striking, calamity overtaking, and being overwhelmed with distress and trouble (1:26). It's so severe it's similar to a storm or a whirlwind. (1:27).

Wisdom will only be good beforehand as prevention, and be no help or cure after the inevitable happens (1:26).That's because life is about cause and effect, and you always end up taking the consequences for your own behaviour in the same way a farmer reaps the harvest he sows (1:31, 11:31, 20:11, 22:8).

Those who don't end up angrily blaming God for their own mistakes (19:3). Your decisions and choices bear fruit over time which you will be forced to eat (1:31). If you heed instruction, you'll profit from it and be rewarded. If you ignore instruction and advice, you'll suffer for it (13:13, 13:18). You may even die (21:16).

You can try to be smart and wise all of your life, searching everywhere and calling out for it, but if you don't fear God, you'll never find it. (1:28-29).

What Character Is

Strength and vigour is the natural advantage of young men, which brings them glory (20:29). Grey hair in men is a glorious sign of a well-lived life, like a crown earned naturally from living the right way as a mark of distinction (16:31, 20:29).

Character is who you are in the dark, when nobody's looking. Nobody likes anyone with a weird, warped mind. They despise them (12:8). Don't try to deceive God or deny what you know. He guards your life and can see everything (24:12).

People aren't generally faithful or loyal, but they always claim to be. It's incredibly hard to find someone who is (20:6).

The nature of someone's character is tested by who they become once they are given fame and praise. In the same way you refine silver in a crucible and gold in a furnace, the pressure of adoration and applause tests who and what you are. (27:21). Your life will reflect your heart in the same way water reflects your face (27:19).

You won't prosper if your motives are bad, and they come from the heart (17:20). The unfaithfulness of duplicity brings ruin (11:3) because it's a trap caused by evil desires (11:6). Pride, arrogance, and haughtiness are an engine and factory for sin (21:4). When you're kind to others, you help yourself; when you're cruel to others, you hurt yourself (11:17).

Be wary and on your guard about your own hypocrisy. Some people are angry at their fathers, but don't do anything good for their mothers; others think of themselves as pure when they are covered in filth; have greedy eyes but glance dismissively at those in need. (30:11-13).

Humble people receive honour for their character and things they achieve. As pride precedes and provokes ruin, the opposite is also true: humility precedes and provokes honour. People pour honour on those who are humble about their success and lowly in spirit (15:33, 18:12, 29:23), and those who loyally defend whom they serve (27:18). Never praise yourself. Let an outsider do it for you (27:2).

What To Live For

What is purpose? What does it mean? Why should you even bother? Our ultimate purpose in life is to glorify God and enjoy Him forever. Everything else is superficial or futile.

> I will say to the north, 'Give them up!' and to the south, 'Do not hold them back'. Bring my sons from afar and my daughters from the ends of the earth - everyone who is called by my name, whom I created for my glory, whom I formed and made.
> *Isaiah 43:6-7*

Excellence

> Whatever your hand finds to do, do it with your might, for there is no work or thought or knowledge or wisdom in Sheol, to which you are going.
> *Ecclesiastes 9:10*

An archer needs a bullseye, as a violinist needs a melody. A builder wants to create a cathedral. To give everything and know you gave all you had.

Beauty

> He has made everything beautiful in its time. He has
> also set eternity in the human heart; yet no one can
> fathom what God has done from beginning to end.
>   *Ecclesiastes 3:11*

There's a flower in the jungle blooming no human will ever lay
eyes on. Why is it there? Why is the girl you love so enchanting
and magical? Why does the orchestra bring you to tears?

Constraining Evil

> When a crime is not punished quickly, people feel it
> is safe to do wrong.
>   *Ecclesiastes 8:11*

Without police, sentries, scouts, or courts, evil runs amok
without end. Unless men confront it, it takes over.

Protectorship

> Defend the cause of the weak and fatherless; main-
> tain the rights of the poor and oppressed. Rescue
> the weak and needy; deliver them from the hand of
> the wicked.
>   *Psalm 82:3-4*

Predators; starvation; exploitation. Natural disasters; expo-
sure; criminality. Neglect, loneliness, and isolation. Injustice,
threats, intimidation. Will you allow it or prevent it?

Adventure

> See, I am doing a new thing! Now it springs up;
> do you not perceive it? I am making a way in the
> wilderness and streams in the wasteland.
> *Isaiah 43:19*

Mountains; deserts; jungles; swamps; ice caps; tundra; oceans. Broken dirt roads, propeller engines; forgotten languages. Storms, dawns, and lost hope. It's out there.

Discovery

> Call to me and I will answer you and tell you great
> and unsearchable things you do not know.
> *Jeremiah 33:3*

Songs need to be written. Mysteries need to be solved. Mathematical formulae and chemical molecules need to be uncovered. Inventions need to be created. Ancient villages and unknown species need to be recorded.

Pioneership

> Those who built on the wall, and those who carried
> burdens, loaded themselves so that with one hand
> they worked at construction, and with the other held
> a weapon. Every one of the builders had his sword
> girded at his side as he built.
> *Nehemiah 4:17-23*

Someone has to be the first to do it and risk everything. Who else will get there and build it? Why not you?

Restoration

> And your ancient ruins shall be rebuilt; you shall raise up the foundations of many generations; you shall be called the repairer of the breach, the restorer of streets to dwell in.
> *Isaiah 58:120*

Spring follows winter and plants regrow out of devastation. Dawn follows night. Wounds heal. The desert blooms. It's never the end. Rebuild it.

Brotherhood

> Though one may be overpowered, two can defend themselves. A cord of three strands is not quickly broken.
> *Ecclesiastes 4:12*

Men don't die for their country. They die to protect the friend next to them.

Stewardship

> The Lord God took the man and put him in the garden of Eden to work it and keep it.
> *Genesis 2:15*

Museums are our memory. Accounts record what we give and owe one another. What is not cared for falls into neglect and ruin.

Fatherhood

> The father of the righteous will greatly rejoice; he
> who fathers a wise son will be glad in him.
> *Proverbs 23:24*

Your son is your reason for all of it; giving him all you never had. History is a contract between the past, present, and future. The hardest and greatest thing you will ever do.

Rescue

> *Rescue those who are being led away to death! Indeed,*
> *hold back those who are staggering to the slaughter.*
> Proverbs 24:11

Have you ever thought of becoming a search and rescue pilot? Are you brave enough to venture into dark caves to find people trapped in there? Could you run into a burning building?

Mastery

> If your sons keep my covenant and the statutes I
> teach them, then their sons will sit on your throne
> for ever and ever.
> *Psalms 132:12*

What is the purpose of becoming excellent at something if not to be a professor to your students and show them how you did it?

Sacrifice

> I heard the voice of the Lord, saying, Whom shall I send, and who will go for us? Then said I, Here am I; send me.
> *Isaiah 6:8*

Give yourself completely to something or someone. Your very life and soul. At full cost to yourself, so that they might live.

God

> Here is the conclusion of the matter: Fear God and keep his commandments, for this is the whole duty of man. For God will bring every deed into judgment, including every hidden thing, whether it is good or evil.
> *Ecclesiastes 12:13-14*

Everything you try to find fulfillment in will fail. Until you serve who created you, for the reason you were created.

II

Types Of People

Human beings easily fall into groups based on their character and how it causes them to behave. It's important to learn what they are, so you know who you are dealing with.

Simple People

All children are born foolish (22:15). Being *Simple* is the stage of adolescence where one is extremely immature and lacks sense; that is, the wisdom gained from life experience. The simple-minded are defined as youthful fools in their natural undeveloped state of folly: gullible, without moral direction, who are inclined to evil by default. This state can persist into late adulthood, but would be most commonly known as the *teenage* years before adult maturity.

In Ancient Hebrew, the words used are *Pethîy* and *Petayim*, which translate to "the simple". The root word from which it is derived, *Pâthâh*, implies extreme vulnerability, literally meaning "to be opened up."

They inherit foolishness and stupidity (14:18), which means they have not gained prudence (8:5), and their lack of sense demands discipline (10:13).

They chase fantasies instead of doing hard work (12:11), their stupidity is contagious (10:17), and they are gullible enough to believe anything (14:15). They are invited to foolishness and death by con artistry (9:14-18). They are especially vulnerable to seduction, lacking an understanding of the irreversible consequences of moral failure (7:6–7).

They see danger, but ignore it and carry on regardless when

they should hide. They end up suffering and paying the price (22:3, 27:12). They die from not growing up out of being on the wrong track (1:32).

If they're still stubborn after dozens of collapses and rebukes, there will come a day when their life simply falls apart, seemingly by surprise, and can't be repaired. There's an endpoint to the mistakes (29:1).

They can change and become wiser if they choose to listen to wise people (21:11). but they take forever to change, because they love the way they are and things they do (1:22). Stupidity brings them joy. It's pleasurable to them (15:21).

The answer to leave their ways behind and choose to walk in wisdom's ways instead (9:6). They sometimes learn to know better if they see an arrogant know-it-all cynic being severely punished (19:25, 21:11), as these people seek out the Simple in order to become their heroes.

Don't rescue them. You'll only have to do it again. Let them suffer the consequences of their actions and learn that way instead (19:19).

If you want to be wise, you need to keep the company of wise people. If your friends are *Simple*, you'll remain that way too (13:20).

At some point, the mistakes you make in your simplicity will mount up to where they are painful. You can ignore reality, but you cannot ignore the *consequences* of ignoring reality. You will be faced with a choice. The goal of loving fatherly discipline is to ensure the choice to pursue wisdom is made as early as possible.

Sarcastic People

Some people are arrogant know-it-all cynics, known as scolds, scorners, *Mockers,* or *Scoffers*. In Ancient Hebrew, the plural used is *Letsîm (Lûwts)*, which translates to "scoffers" from the verb *Lyts ("to scoff", or "to make mouths at")*. Scorning fools utterly detests people and ideas that contradict their false thinking, and they express their scorn through derisive attitudes, behavior, and speech.

They are proud and arrogant, and live in a pattern of erupting in insolent, self-righteous fury (21:24). They find joy in looking down at others and mocking them (1:22). Many of these individuals are to be found in the bourgeois upper and upper-middle classes, in professions such as journalism.

People hate and detest them (24:9). Their insults and arguments stir up entire cities with bad feeling and conflict (29:8).

They try to find wisdom but never succeed (14:6). They resent being corrected by anyone, which means they avoid wise people (15:12). If you try to correct one, you're asking for a barrage of insults in return (9:7). If you rebuke them, they will hate you (9:8), ignore it, and not respond (13:1).

God mocks them and their pride (3:34).

Punishments are lined up for them (19:29). If you punish

them severely in public, and it might shock and warn simple people into being more conscientious about the way they live (19:25). Get rid of them and you'll get rid of the fighting caused by their behaviour (22:10).

If you keep the company of mockers and scoffers, you'll become one of them. Avoid them (13:20).

Lazy People

Some people are lazy, slovenly gluttons, known as *Sluggards*. Or, humans with the characteristics and mobility of a garden slug. In Ancient Hebrew, the adjective used is *Atsel*, which translates to "slothful", "indolent", or "sluggish, lazy". Indolent fools possess a different form of offensive pride.

Their house is overgrown with weeds and thorns from neglect, with crumbling walls falling to pieces (24:31). They lie in their bed rolling over like the hinge of a door (26:14). They make up completely ridiculous excuses not to even leave the house, like it being a life-threatening risk of a lion loose in the street outside (22:13, 26:13). Some are so lazy they won't even lift their gluttonous arm out of a plate of food to feed themselves (19:24, 26:15).

They are completely convinced of their own cleverness. So convinced, they believe they are smarter than seven wise people combined (26:16). Yet they have no sense, even if they inherit wealth or have the means to generate it (24:30).

They don't do the work they should at the normal times they should, so they go hungry despite searching for food (20:4) and miss out on luxurious things and lovely foods (12:27). Their appetite is never satisfied or fulfilled (13:4) and they are always hungry with no work to keep them busy (19:15) — which they wouldn't do anyway (20:4). Their life is a slow, difficult, almost-impossible struggle through painful obstacles, like trying to fight through thorns (15:19). It's this 24/7 craving is what leads to their self-destructive death because of their own refusal to satiate it through hard work (21:25-26)..

Laziness is infectious (10:17) and it will make you sleep deeply (19:15, 20:13). It will make you poor (10:4, 20:13). Don't sleep too much. Definitely don't nap on the job. It will destroy any chance you have of prosperity, fast. Poverty will hit you so quickly it will be like a thief attacking you; an armed robber holding you up and stealing everything you have (6:9-11). Even taking small day-naps folding your hands over your chest means poverty will strip you like an armed robber (24:33-34).

It will end up with you doing hard unskilled work you hate because you have no other choice (12:24)

If you are slack in your work, you let down your friends and colleagues. It's destructive to others and like a form of vandalism (18:7). Sleeping when it is time to harvest is disgraceful (10:5). Lazy people are so obnoxious to employers they are like the taste of raw vinegar, or smoke in the eyes (10:26).

If you keep the company of lazy people, you'll become one of them. Avoid them (13:20).

If you're lazy, the answer is to use the ant as a model example to fix yourself. Copy what it does. It doesn't need to be told what to do by someone else and uses its own initiative. It stores up supplies during summer, so it has a huge stockpile to harvest before winter (6:6-8).

Stupid People

All children are born foolish. All humans start their existence as fools, and no-one is exempted. It is the natural state of humanity from our first moments. The job of parents is to forcibly remove it from us with the love of harsh discipline (22:15). If a child receives none, or no wisdom is learned, a person won't leave this state (22:6).

Some people are terminally stupid and reckless by character, regardless of their age. Not simply immature or lacking experience, but irrationally subjugated by their own ignorance, and persistently stubborn in their own prideful refusal to accept correction of any kind. They are known as *Fools*, or people entirely deficient in moral reasoning.

In Ancient Hebrew, different words are used. *Kisîlim (kecîyl)* is used the most, which translates to "fool" or "dullard"; someone who rejects Godly living for glorying in shameful sensual pleasures. The other word, E*vîlîm (eviyl)* tends to refer to "fool" in the sense of a person who is silly or insincere; an arrogant, impulsive back-chatter with a big mouth.

You will recognise these adult children as being extremely common on social media and reality TV. It could be said we live in a culture of Fools.

They despise the idea of being wise, and are implicitly

atheistic. They refuse to accept or follow instruction (1:7), and stubbornly hate turning away from evil (13:19). Their hearts are empty and wired wrongly in favour of it (15:7). They hate knowledge (1:22) and find no pleasure in it (18:2). Them quoting wise sayings is idiotic. It's as insightful as the useless legs of a cripple (26:7) or thorns in a drunk's hand (26:9).

They make their stupidity obvious and leave a mess everywhere (13:16). It is contagious (10:17). They feed on stupidity, slander, gossip, and trash as if it were food at a banquet (15:14).

The ultimate cause of their demise is deception: being easily deceived, and deceiving themselves (14:8). The core of the problem is self-delusion. If you deceive yourself; believing yourself to be in the right, there's more hope for a fool than you (26:12). A Fool's complacency and self-assurance ends up completely destroying their lives. Their lack of sense will physically kill them. (1:32, 8:36, 10:21). They rip their own home down with their own hands (14:1), and the inheritance they earn is shame (3:35).

They are volatile and hot-headed, yet completely confident in their stupidity (14:17). They don't hold back or restrain the full extent of their arrogant rage and lash out immediately (29:11, 14:3), flaring up in irritated anger the second they feel annoyed (12:16). They loudly blurt out all their thoughts and feelings instead of being discrete (12:23), and erupt into arguing and quarreling almost instantly (20:3).

Their greedy eyes constantly wander everywhere (17:24). When they have plenty to eat they are insufferable (30:22). They impulsively and gluttonously shove the best foods down their neck without thinking (21:20).

Their mouth is what brings them to ruin (10:14) because

they only ever speak stupidity (15:2). The things they say are so stupid they practically invite a beating and only ever bring them trouble and ruin, even killing them (18:6-7). They are unruly and loud (9:13-15), chattering away (10:8, 10:10) spreading slander (10:18). Everything they say is perverse (19:1), and they take pleasure both in evil scheming (24:9), as well as publicly broadcasting their opinions (10:23, 18:2). Speaking eloquently is unnatural to them (17:7), and their constant lies are the way they conceal their arrogant hatred (10:18).

If they're committed to their stupidity, they'll be so aggressive towards you stopping them it's like a mother bear defending her young. If you try to intervene, you'll get mauled (17:12). Their stupidity generates more stupidity. It doesn't build anything or yield a return or profit. It merely produces more and more stupidity (14:24). At which point they will repeat their own stupidity mindlessly like a dog returning to eat its own vomit (26:11).

They hate being corrected (12:1). If you correct or rebuke them, you will be met with extreme hostility (9:7-8). They ignore advice and refuse to listen to it, because they are convinced they know best (12:15). They disown and reject the discipline their parents try to apply (15:5).

If you hire one, they will injure everyone around them like an archer shooting and wounding at random (26:10). Using them to relay messages is so perilous it's like cutting off your own feet or drinking poison (26:6).

If you take them to court, they rage angrily, scoff and mock, and give no-one any peace (29:9). They mock the idea of making amends for wronging someone (14:9).

Honouring them is totally inappropriate and honour is

completely alien to them, like snow in summer or rain during harvest (26:1). It's so counter-productive it's like tying a stone into a sling (26:8). They are completely out of place in luxurious circumstances they couldn't even earn by themselves honestly (19:10).

Not responding to the extreme way they provoke you is a heavy burden like sand or a massive stone. (27:3). Don't respond to their stupidity, or you'll become just like them. Answer them simply in a way a stupid person would understand or they'll end up congratulating themselves (26:4-5). It's pointless to speak to them as they'll dismiss anything good you have to say (23:9).

Endless beatings lie in store for them as their fate (19:29) because their stupidity invites and brings them punishment (16:22). Getting told off and beaten up is as natural to them as a horse taking a whip or a donkey wearing a saddle (26:3). You can lash them a hundred times and they still won't learn (17:10).

Don't rescue them. You'll only have to do it again. Let them suffer the consequences of their actions and learn that way instead (19:19). You cannot remove their stupidity from them even by grinding them in a mortar, or treating them like grain in a pestle (27:22).

Wisdom is too much for them. When it's important or there's a crisis, they must not be allowed to speak (24:7).

If you spend time with them, you will become like them (13:20). Stay away from them at all costs. There is nothing they can teach you or help you with, nothing to learn from them (14:7).

Evil People

Some people are evil. They are *godless*, or *Wicked*. Although they are still categorised as fools, their folly is something darker: an arrogant moral abyss; a complete lack of righteousness, deriving pleasure from selfish cruelty. In Ancient Hebrew, the adverb used is *Rasha*, which translates to "morally wrong, bad, or wicked person"; whereas the noun is *Nâbâl*, translated as "stupid, wicked" or "vile person".

It is their goal to draw as many others as possible into their evil ways. Attempts to reprove them will be futile and bring frustration to the one who tries to influence them. Only God can successfully reprove steadfastly evil fools.

The sexes express evil differently. Men abuse their strength to tyrannise and steal (1:12), whereas women abuse their sexuality to betray (2:16-17). They started well, but then chose to walk down the wrong road (2:13, 2:17, 12:26, 14:22. 28:10, 28:14) because of foolishness.

The root cause is a lack of discipline (5:23, 28:4) which leads them into a world which gets ever darker (4:19) in rebellion against God (17:11). In some circumstances, it's because the people they followed listened to lies (29:12).

Corrupting people is easier than you imagine; they will do evil for a meal or a small gift (28:21). It can be expunged and purged from someone's character with extremely severe punishment (20:30). Otherwise, they will inevitably gain a reputation as a schemer (24:8).

If you look for evil, you'll get it and it will invade your life (11:27). Shame and contempt always follows it (18:3). Never, never, never get involved with evil or criminal people in any way. Never, ever be tempted to accept their invitation when they seek you out. (1:10) Go out of your way to avoid them and don't allow yourself to cross paths with them (3:7, 4:14). Don't take one step in their direction. (1:15, 4:15) This is a life and death decision. (1:19).

Evil people relish doing evil and run to do it as their sustenance (1:16, 2:14, 4:17, 19:28, 21:10). They take bribes in secret to ruin justice (17:23, 29:4), which they hate (21:15). They're hungry (13:25) and restless and can't sleep until they've harmed someone and suffer insomnia (4:16). They put up a bold front (21:29), work quickly, harm others quickly (1:16), speak evil quickly (15:28, 24:2), and can't understand why they suffer disaster (4:19, 11:8, 12:21, 22:5, 24:16) because of their refusal to do what's right (21:7, 22:8) or even understand what it is (28:5).

Their words and speech are charming (26:25) but vile (2:12, 6:12, 13:5, 24:2) and overflow with concealed violence (10:6, 10:11, 12:6, 26:24-26) which can destroy entire civilisations (11:11, 29:4) and traps them (12:13). They rejoice in how perverse evil is (2:14), have empty industry which produces sin (21:4), and their heart isn't of much value (10:20, 24:2). They know they are attacking innocent people and they're devious. (1:11, 2:15, 12:20) They certainly don't care about the poor (29:7) and they really hate Godly virtuous people so much they seek to murder them (29:10, 29:27).

They try to tempt you with plans which they claim will be foolproof, pleasurable, and net you a share of what they steal. (1:12-14, 27:6). They recruit simple people who live close by and lead them astray (16:29, 21:10, 28:10); they're easy targets because they lack self-discipline and easily praise the wrong people (28:4). They signal their evil intent by winking maliciously (10:10, 16:30), clenching their lips (16:30), as well as making signs with their fingers and feet (6:13). What they take from others will overwhelm and kill them (1:19, 15:6, 21:7) and the things they do trap them like an animal locked inescapably in a snare (5:22, 21:7, 26:27, 29:6, 29:24) or lead them to fall into a deep hole (28:18).

If a good person gives in them, they're like a muddied or polluted well (25:26). If you try to correct one, you will receive abuse (9:7). Their advice is deceitful (12:4), they listen to liars (17:4), and even their kindest acts are cruel (12:10, 27:6). When they get into office or leadership, it drives ordinary people into hiding (28:12, 28:28), the population collapses into widespread sin (29:16), and they moan with misery (29:2).

Murderers, for example, are tormented by guilt and seek refuge in the relief they believe they will also die. There's no hope or remedy for them. Don't get in their way or stop them getting their wish (28:17).

Don't envy them (3:31, 23:17, 24:1, 24:19), worry over them (24:19), or show them favouritism (18:5). All people who try to gain by criminal means end up dying younger than expected (10:27, 13:9). Even just trying to. (1:19) They stir up trouble and conflict (6:14, 24:1) and have no hope in life (10:28, 11:23, 24:20). Evil is a one-way suicide mission where they are broadcasting their nature to everyone, and being the person who hunts and traps themselves (1:17-18, 11:5, 13:6,

21:18, 22:5, 28:10, 29:6, 29:24)

If you join them, you will die (1:19, 3:31, 11:19. 24:1) because their deceptive wages are sin and death (10:16, 11:18). They are always fleeing and looking over their shoulder because of their paranoia; even though no-one is chasing them (28:1).

And if somehow they survive, their destiny is to be cut off and ruined (2:22, 10:30, 11:20, 12:7, 14:11, 17:11) so their reputation rots (10:7) and they are made to bow before good people (14:19) by leaders looking to get rid of them for everyone's benefit (20:8, 20:26). They are often brought down by Godly people who notice them and resist what they are up to (21:12, 28:4) and if they corrupt good people, they will fall into their own trap (27:10).

They cannot be established (12:3) in the stronghold they want (12:12) , so the inevitable disaster which they dread catches up with them (10:24, 13:21, 14:32-33) and is always sudden, instant, and irreversible (6:15, 10:25, 24:20, 29:16). Justice against them causes everyone to celebrate with shouts of joy (11:10, 21:15, 28:28, 29:6), especially when their means of angrily harming others is neutralised (22:8).

God hates them, curses them, and their home (3:33, 10:29, 15:8-9). He rejects their self-serving religious cries to Him (21:27), exposes them (10:9, 26:26), hates their thoughts (15:26), condemns their schemes (12:2), and blocks them from having what their appetites crave (10:3, 22:12).

If you keep the company of evil people, you'll become one of them. Avoid them, because your life genuinely does depends on it (13:20).

Godly People

No-one can say they're truly good or haven't sinned (20:9). However, a minority of people deliberately set down the narrowest path to serve God and chase after wisdom, after having renounced foolishness. They are rare, and known as the *Righteous, Blameless,* or *Upright.*

The word used in Ancient Hebrew is *Yasar,* which translates to "straight", "vertically erect", "horizontally level or smooth", or "evenly distributed". It means to be free of blemish or corruption, and have God's stamp of approval. Their key characteristics are integrity and righteousness.

Good is defined by God's thinking and standards, not our own (3:7, 19:16). It means what is morally right, just, and fair (2:9), which Godly people understand intuitively (27:5). Seeking it will bring you favour (11:27). Those who do end up finding love and faithfulness (14:22); life, prosperity, and honour (21:21); living lives free of blame which straighten the road for their children (20:7). The end of the road leads to eternal life with God (12:28).

What righteous Godly people want ends up in their good, and the good of those around them (11:23). When good people prosper, everyone around them benefits and celebrates (11:10, 11:11, 28:12, 28:28, 29:2). Their integrity can lift up entire countries (14:34). Their life bears wonderful fruit (11:30, 12:28) and they leave a healthy inheritance for their grandchildren (13:22).

Godly people keep secrets faithfully and are trustworthy (11:13). They think through their behaviour in detail (21:29), as well as consider and weigh what they intend to say before blurting things out (15:28). If you rebuke them, they listen and learn (19:25).

Upright people love justice and celebrate it because it sparks joy for them (21:15), particularly when the poor receive it fairly (29:7). They care for the lowest among us, like animals (12:10), and hate evil people. They make notes of them and bring them to ruin (21:12, 29:27). They are discerning about who they have as friends (12:26) and they can see through the delusions of the rich (28:11).

In the grand scheme of things, Godly mediators with integrity and patience, who are self-controlled, are more useful and effective than lethal warriors who can take a whole city (16:32). Patience itself is a product of wisdom (19:11).

Good people give and give without thinking about holding back portions for themselves (21:26, 22:9). A quick way to mimic their kindness is not to hold back help if it's within your means, and the person deserves it. If you can help, do it. (3:27).

The lives of people who love God and try to live rightly get better and better as they age (4:18, 15:24), it gains them favour from Him (12:2, 13:9, 15:8), they are as a bold and confident as a lion (28:1), and they live free from punishment (11:21, 15:24). Their plans are just (12:5) and they hate what is false (13:5). Their good words save them when they get stuck (12:6) because of the good will they generate (14:9), and keep them out of trouble (12:13, 28:18, 28:26). They run to God for rescue and shelter in every single circumstance, even their own death (14:32), and manage to get back up seven times over (24:16). He loves them (15:9) and blesses them with a lovely inheritance (28:10).

Righteousness will save your life (10:2, 11:4, 12:21, 15:24), help you thrive (11:28, 13:21, 14:11) like a healthy plant that continually provides wealthy fruit (12:12, 15:6), give you the hope of future joy (10:28), straighten your path into a highway avoiding evil (11:5, 15:19, 15:21, 16:17), and the wages of it are life (10:16, 11:19, 22:4). It will even help you save other people's lives (11:30) and let you eat as much as you want (13:25).

Living with integrity will guide and guard you (11:3, 13:6, 16:17), bring you the rescue of refuge and security (10:9, 10:29, 11:8), provide you resilience from storms (10:25, 11:5, 12:7, 24:16) so you are never uprooted (10:30, 12:3), and ensure what you desire will be granted (10:24).

Don't put your hope in men. All the hope goes when they die. Their power means nothing (11:7, 29:25). Good people who give in to evil people are like a polluted, muddy well (25:26).

It's better to do what's right, just, and fair than try to make any kind of bargain with God or undertake any theatrical performance for Him (21:3). You'll be repaid for what you give. If you're mean, you'll be repaid in full with nothing. If you're kindhearted and Godly, you'll be rewarded with that. (14:15). God orders and progresses the big picture of your short life on Earth even if you organise the day-to-day things (16:9). If He approves and intervenes in your life, even your enemies will show you greetings and favour (16:7).

III

Strategy

Once you understand what the different paths are
and who people can be grouped into, the question is:
how should you live? What is the best way to live?

Emotional Health

Humans are spiritual beings. Our soul is like a lamp God placed inside us which illuminates who we truly are at our deepest depth (20:27). Your heart and soul are broad and deep. It's hard to know what drives you and what you want, or what gives you a sense of meaning and purpose. If you're wise, you can understand yourself and be perceptive about others (20:5).

Everything in your life flows from your heart. Guard it. (4:23). Your life will reflect your heart in the same way water reflects your face (27:19). You won't prosper if your motives are bad, and they come from the heart (17:20).

If you fail, flounder, or collapse when it counts - when there's a storm of trouble - your weakness is an embarrassment (24:10).

The key to success in life is self-control. If you're impulsive, explosive, or otherwise lack it, you're as vulnerable as a strong fortress citadel whose walls have been broken through. Your defenses are down and you will be routed by people looking to overcome you (25:28).

Emotional health and peace of mind are a product of wisdom: it will enable you to live in safety, feel at ease, and not worry about being harmed (1:33, 3:23). It protects and guards you (2:11, 4:6, 6:22, 9:12) to give you hope and peace (3:2,

23:18), brings you an inheritance of honour (3:35, 4:8), and is spiritually pleasant (2:10, 3:17). It will protect your physical body (3:8, 3:22, 4:22), help you sleep well at night without anxiety or nightmares (3:24), extend your life expectancy (4:10,7:2, 9:11,10:27), and make you prosperous (3:2, 19:8). You won't have to fear sudden disaster or ruin (3:25, 4:12, 23:18).

If your heart is peaceful, and your life is peaceful, you'll see it in your physical appearance. You'll look healthy and display vitality (14:30) and wear a smile on your face (15:13). If you're optimistic and positive, your heart will have a constant feast (15:15). Promoting peace will bring you joy (12:20). Eat good, healthy foods and enjoy their taste (24:13). When you're kind to others, you help yourself; when you're cruel to others, you hurt yourself (11:17).

A miserable, mean heart means a miserable life 15:15). If you burn with resentment and envy, it'll feel like your bones are rotting inside you (14:30). Don't swear revenge or payback (24:29). Pride, arrogance, and haughtiness are an engine and factory for sin (21:4). Hardening your heart, or turning against God, will send you down the wrong road land you in trouble (28:14).

Everyone has their own pain and joy only they feel and experience. Yours won't be the same as others, and vice versa (14:10). The people you see laughing may well be devastated and heartbroken inside. And some days, celebrations may ironically end in tragedy (14:13).

Your emotions and spirit are intimately linked. If you're heartbroken, your spirit will feel crushed (15:13). It can feel like it's deep in your bones and they've dried up (17:23). It feels unbearable (18:14). Anxiety and worry weighs your heart down (12:25). Hope for something which keeps being put off as a relentless disappointment makes you sick and depressed (13:12).

When you finally get something you want out of nowhere, it refreshes your life and vitality (13:12) and it feels sweet to your soul (13:19). Seeing a happy face with a cheerful heart brightens anyone up like a powerful medicine (15:13, 17:22). Lovely smells and lotions bring joy to the heart (27:9). Good news goes down into your bones and makes you feel physically healthier and stronger (15:30); it's like cold, refreshing water in the desert to someone with a weary soul (25:25).

The nature of someone's character is tested by who they become once they are given fame and praise. In the same way you refine silver in a crucible and gold in a furnace, the pressure of adoration and applause tests who you are (27:21).

Speech

God spoke the universe into existence (Gen 1:3) in the beginning; the Word was with Him and was Him (John 1:1). His speech is wisdom; knowledge and understanding (2:6).

Language is complex and is a deep and broad reservoir of communication (18:4). Words are inflammatory and hold the power of life and death. They can kill or give life. Either way, the consequences of how you use, misuse, or abuse them will be experienced and evident in your life (18:21).

Listen first. Don't cut someone off or provide the answer before hearing the situation or question (18:13). The first person to speak always seems right, until what they say is scrutinised by the next person to speak after them (18:17). Keep your own counsel and your cards close to your chest. Don't boast or over-share (12:23).

Speaking quickly or explosively is so foolish, there's more hope for the stupidest idiot than someone who allows themselves to (29:20). Truthful speech is impactful and is remembered for a lifetime (12:19). Good speech helps virtuous people escape trouble (12:6), but bad speech and double-talk will trap you in it (12:13, 12:20). To be wise, hold your tongue (10:19, 11:12) and only use it when your words will find favour and be received well (10:32). Restraint will save you from inadvertent disaster (21:23), and could save your life (13:3). Consider and weigh what you intend to say (15:28). Even a fool looks thoughtful and discerning if he stays quiet or restrains his response (17:28).

Certain types of speech are not wanted or expected from different people (17:7). Wise people are differentiated from Fools by how they use it. Be careful of what you say and be mindful of the words others hear from out of your mouth. Don't use bad, nasty, or corrupt language like white lies and gossip. Keep it hygienically clean (4:24). Misusing it to avoid offense with long words and long obscure vocabulary doesn't change anything (10:19). It's better to be poor and honest than lie or speak in a disgusting way (19:1, 19:22).

Evil people use it for violence (10:6, 24:2) to destroy others (11:9) or for concealing violence (10:10, 26:24) because it's all they know to use it for (10:32). Their mouth gushes with evil (15:28, 26:24) and it is like a fire which scorches and burns what it touches (16:27). It's a tool for disguising their true intent, which is harbouring deceit (26:24). Words spoken by someone with an evil heart are like a glaze of painted silver on an empty clay vase (26:23). Evil words and speech end up being silenced (10:31).

Promiscuous women use their words in a seductive way (2:16, 7:5, 7:21). Female sexual predators know what to say to reel in simple fools, and they're smooth (5:3, 6:24, 22:14).

Fools use it for chattering, which brings them to ruin (10:10, 13:3). The stupid things they say inevitably invite it (10:14), as does their arrogant lashing out (14:3). Their prideful, impulsive, and intemperate verbal stupidity invites ruin, beatings, and even their death (18:6-7). Don't waste your time speaking to them. They won't listen (23:9).

Don't gossip (11:13), slander (10:18), tattle (11:13), or lie (10:18). In the short term it feels wonderful, like a tasty meal (18:8, 26:22) which goes right down well and smoothly (26:22), but ultimately it separates close friends (16:28) and stirs conflict (26:20). People who gossip betray the confidential trust of others and are treacherous. Be wary of talkers (20:19). Sly cynical chatter will earn you horrified looks from people. It's like a wind from the north bringing unexpected stormy rain (25:23).

Liars love listening to gossip and lies (17:4), which only last a few seconds before they are dismissed or forgotten (12:19). Lying and false testimony will get you into a lot of trouble. You'll be found out, be punished, and imprisoned. You might even lose your life (11:5, 11:9). Don't use your speech to mislead others with false testimony about someone who hasn't wronged you (24:28).

Don't flatter people, and be suspicious of flattery in general. Someone who flatters you is setting you up, spreading a net underneath your feet (29:5-6). Flattery is a destructive form of lying which is hateful in nature (26:28). It's more fruitful to rebuke someone openly in public than to only express your love to someone in private where it's hidden (27:5). When all is said and done, it will earn you favour you wouldn't have had if you'd flattered them (28:23).

Don't make grandiose proclamations, like swearing revenge on someone publicly (20:22), or boasting confidently about what tomorrow will bring (27:1). Don't boast about giving gifts you never have. People who do are like clouds and wind missing rain. They're empty and pointless (25:14). If you want an important person to want to be friends with you, speak gracefully, and make clear your love of good people with pure motives (22:11).

Speech comes from the heart. Wise, smart people give good advice and demand instruction be followed because they have wisdom living in their hearts (16:23). Words from a godly person are like the rushing stream of a beautiful fountain (18:4), providing life and refreshment (10:11, 15:2, 15:4), like the best kind of silver (10:20), or a rare jewel (20:15) because their lips deliver wisdom and its fruits (10:13, 10:31). They are used with restraint (17:28), to nourish large amounts of people (10:21) and protect (14:3) by providing knowledge, instruction, and prudence (15:7).

God loves gracious words (15:26). Kind, soothing speech is sweet like a honeycomb, and words used in the right way can fill people with pleasure and satisfaction (12:14, 13:2); cheering up people who feel anxious or depressed like a medicine (12:25), and healing people if used to provide wisdom and counsel (12:18), even physically deep as into their bones (16:24).

Good conversation feels wonderful. The right words at the right time are pure joy (15:23), and an honest answer is like a kiss on the lips (24:26). The right words come from God (16:1) and they satisfy the mind like food from a prosperous harvest fills up your stomach (18:20).

Giving instructions graciously means they are more likely to be followed (16:22). But you will need more than tough talk to get people to respond (29:19).

Nasty, vile speech can crush a person's morale and spirit (15:4). If you use words recklessly they pierce a person like a sword (12:18) and ignite quarrels (15:1). If someone is angry with you, speak gently back in a meek voice to calm them down (15:1).

Good Faith

Good faith and good will are a by-product and mark of someone trying to live in a Godly way (14:9). Duplicity brings ruin (11:3). as does approaching situations in bad faith (13:15). People deceive themselves about their own goodness and their good faith (16:2). When you're kind to others, you help yourself; when you're cruel to others, you might be able to make a fortune (11:16) but you hurt yourself (11:17). Innocent people can be identified by the Godliness of their ordinary life (21:8), and vice versa. Choose wisdom, not scheming (10:23).

God weighs and measures our hearts (21:2, 24:12) and can't be deceived (24:12). He examines our internal motives (16:2, 20:27, 21:2, 24:12), and the subsequent choices we make (5:21, 20:27). You won't prosper if your motives are bad, and they come from the heart (17:20). Even children display questionable motives (20:11). God is the lawyer of those who are poor, and He will stand up for them if you treat them wrongly (21:13, 28:27).

In all of your dealings, speak gracefully (4:24), show patience (14:29, 19:11) and promote peace (12:20), because love covers all wrongs (10:12). Speak gently to soothe anger and defensiveness (15:1), and give an gift honestly (18:16). Listen first. Don't cut someone off or provide the answer before hearing the situation or question (18:13). Keep secrets faithfully and be trustworthy (11:13). Humility will bring you wisdom (11:2), and kindheartedness will bring honour (11:16) which benefits you (11:17). Seeking righteousness will bring you favour (11:27) and lead to others refreshing you in return (11:25). A good reputation and receiving good will arise from your love and faithfulness (3:4), and leaders specifically look at motives (16:13, 22:11).

Give without thinking about holding back portions for yourself (21:26, 22:9). Don't hold back help if it's within your means, and the person deserves it. If you can help, do it (3:27). Being stingy and mean won't help you prosper, it will bring you to ruin (28:22).

Don't use dishonest scales or measurements (11:1, 16:11, 20:10, 20:23). Bad work gets paid with a bad check; good work gets solid pay (11:18). Don't offer bribes (17:8) or take bribes. It'll cost you your life (15:27). Pull your weight. Being lazy is destructive to others and like a form of vandalism (18:7). If you hire a fool, they will randomly injure everyone around them (26:10). The wrong messenger can ruin all your best efforts (13:17).

People hate and detest arrogant cynics, so be careful of how you appear to others (24:9). The insults and arguments from cynics and critics stir up entire cities with bad feeling and conflict (29:8). Nobody likes anyone with a weird, warped mind (12:8).

Don't gossip (11:13, 20:19), slander (10:18), tattle (11:13), pick arguments (17:14), lie (10:18), or boast about gifts you haven't given (25:14). Sly chat will earn you bad looks from others (25:23). Don't defame a loyal worker or good employee to their boss. They'll condemn you and punish you for it.

(30:10). If you protect your boss, you'll receive honor (27:18), as you will for expressing your affection for people with good motives (22:11).

Don't react instantly or rise to the bait (12:16, 19:11, 20:3). Don't rise to being unnecessarily or unfairly insulted when you never deserved it (26:2).

Don't lead people on (3:28) or take vows lightly or impulsively (20:25). That means deceiving people and then claiming to have just been joking. It's like a madman shooting flaming arrows of death (26:18-19). Don't delay returning things unnecessarily, delay repayment (3:28), or withhold what you can give (11:24, 11:26).

Don't deride people who live nearby and trust you (11:12), plot against them (3:29), or make baseless accusations about people who have not harmed you (3:30, 24:28). If you dream up evil schemes, you will be hated for it (14:17). If you try to intervene to stop stupid people behaving foolishly, expect to be mauled (17:12) and met with hostility (9:7-8).

Tell the truth as a witness, and do not lie to create a smokescreen (12:17, 14:5). Don't crush vulnerable people in court (22:22), nor condemn the innocent or acquit the guilty (17:15, 24:24). You'll be cursed by entire peoples and condemned by entire countries (24:24). Don't show partiality or favouritism to evil people because it deprives the innocent of justice (18:5, 28:21). Fools will only ever act in bad faith if you take them to court (29:9).

Be aware of flatterers. They're acting in bad faith and softening you up (29:5). People cover up their ulterior bad motives with kisses (27:6). Riches will attract fake friends (14:20, 19:4) who are only there for the freebies (11:6). Know the kind of character you are dealing with (19:19).

If you've screwed up, 'fess up. If you're in a hole, stop digging. Don't try covering up, or digging yourself out (28:13).

Don't be jealous of those who get their way by hurting others (3:31). If you sow injustice, you'll reap ruin and disaster for yourself (22:8). If you pay back evil for good, or bad faith for good faith, evil will never leave you or your home. You've ensnared yourself without knowing (17:13). Cruelty will bring you ruin (11:17), as will gloating after you've won (24:17).

Recognise others behaving in bad faith. All the different types of fool will rarely act in good faith. But in particular, evil people - the *Wicked* and the *Adulteress* - are characterised by their refusal to, and in how they signal their treacherous intent (5:4, 6:13, 7:11, 10:10, 16:30, 23:27). Do not deal with them (23:9).

Anger & Conflict

Conflict rarely appears out of nowhere. It is caused by specific personality types and identifiable disagreements. Wherever you find it, the root problem is always the same: *pride* (13:10).

Conflict is caused by hatred (10:12), as well as angry (29:22) or hot-tempered people (15:18); but mostly, greed and the need to obtain more of one's desires (28:25). If you speak to someone harshly, you'll make them angry and defensive (15:1). Gossip also causes problems between people who are close (16:28), and jealousy is a wild madness of emotion which is harder to deal with than any other behaviour (27:4).

Unfaithful people have an appetite for conflict (13:2), and evil, twisted people like to incite it (6:14, 16:28). Loners and unfriendly people are selfish. They spurn the necessity of relationships with others and often deliberately pick fights (18:1). People aren't generally faithful or loyal, but they always claim to be. It's incredibly hard to find someone who is (20:6).

Deliberately stirring up anger is guaranteed to cause division and bad feeling. It's like churning cream to make butter or twisting someone's nose to break it (30:33). Anger ends in cruelty (27:4) because fury overwhelms a person (27:4). It will affect your body and be visible (14:30). so to counter it, wise people reject it and turn it away (29:8).

Being hot-tempered will cause you to do and say stupid things (14:17). If you like fighting and quarreling, the real problem is you love sin. If you go out there advertising you are ready for a fight, you're inviting ruin (17:19). Deliberately picking a fight is like smashing open a dam. Drop the issue before the fight starts (17:14). Don't rescue hot-tempered people. You'll only have to do it again. Let them suffer the consequences of their actions and learn that way instead (19:19).

Don't become too over-familiar with other people's homes. Don't visit too often or hang around too much. They'll hate you for it. (25:17).

Don't join, associate with, or ally with political rebels, troubles, or revolutionaries. God and the leaders they fight against will ruin them quickly in surprise attacks. You don't know how deep that trouble will go (24:21-22).

Don't get involved in an argument which has nothing to do with you. You're asking for trouble, like grabbing a mad stray dog by the ears (26:17). Probing too deeply into painful things can end up in you covered in dirt or dishonour (25:27). Avoid arguments and trouble if you possibly can as it's the honourable way of dealing with them, Don't react instantly or rise to the bait (12:16, 19:11, 20:3). Don't rise to being unnecessarily or unfairly insulted when you never deserved it. You have nothing to fear. It's as fleeting as a tiny bird which doesn't land (26:2).

Be patient. If you fly off the handle and lose your temper easily, you'll look stupid (14:29). If you're patient and overlook an offence, your glory will be on display (19:11). The first person to speak always seems right. Until what they say is scrutinised by their opponent (18:17). Wise people finalise and end conflicts by calming things down and bringing peace (29:11). It's calmed by patient middlemen and mediators who don't react and wait for the anger to relent (15:18, 19:11)

Arguments and fights need fuel to continue or restart, as fires need wood or charcoal. Their fuel is gossip and the aggressive behaviour of high-conflict people. Take away the fuel and the fire will go out. (26:20-21). High-conflict troublemakers like cynics, complainers, and sarcastic bullies are often the source of arguments and insults which incubate fighting. Get rid of them and peace will return (22:10).

An offended close friend won't give in or lower their guard. They are so entrenched they are like a city in a war protecting itself (18:19), but love and faithfulness make amends for injuries (16:7). To calm someone down who is angry, speak in a soft, gentle voice (15:1), and to soothe someone who is *extremely* angry, give them a gift in secret; a financial bundle will definitely change their mood (21:14). If multiple parties can't agree, roll a dice and use randomness for allocation and priorities to soothe the friction (18:18).

Choose middlemen who relay messages for you carefully. An evil one will bring trouble, and but one you can trust heals the situation (13:17). Light in their eyes will bring happiness and joy to the recipient (15:30). Their trustworthiness and integrity refreshes the sender's spirit like a cold drink of snow water in the heat of harvest (25:13).

Don't publicise that you'll take revenge. Let God avenge you. (20:22), but don't gloat or rejoice when your enemies lose because God will see and give them a break. (24:17). If your enemy is hungry, feed him. If he's thirsty, give him a drink. Your goodness will take him completely by surprise and earn God's favour towards you. It's like throwing burning coals over his head, all for you to get the reward for discontinuing the conflict (25:21-22).

If conflict and confrontation is unavoidable, and you have to go to war as a last resort, get advice and guidance. Get lots of it (20:18, 24:6). Do not crush vulnerable *or* needy people in court. God will become their lawyer and judge against you (22:22).

IV

Dangers

Everything might be possible, but it's not always profitable or healthy. There are constraints which must be applied to specific areas of one's life.

Pleasures

Hedonism, or the pursuit of pleasure, is pointless and empty (20:17). Seeking it and loving it will guarantee you poverty (21:17). However, all these things are a by-product of diligent hard work (10:6, 28:20, 2:27).

The nature of someone's character is tested by who they become once they are given fame and praise. In the same way you refine silver in a crucible and gold in a furnace, the pressure of adoration and applause tests who you are. (27:21).

Sin doesn't discriminate. It condemns anyone and everyone, and even entire countries (14:34). Don't let you eyes wander everywhere. Stay focused (17:24). If you see danger, hide, run, avoid, or get away from it. Find refuge (22:3, 27:12).

Strength and vigour is the natural advantage of young men, which brings them glory (20:29). Grey hair in men is a glorious sign of a well-lived life, like a crown earned naturally from living the right way as a mark of distinction (16:31, 20:29).

Death and destruction are never, ever satisfied. They always want more and more company (27:20). If you're impulsive, explosive, or otherwise lack self-control, you're as vulnerable as a strong fortress citadel whose walls have been broken through. Your defenses are down and you will be routed by people looking to overcome you. (25:28)

Discipline is what will save you or keep you as a fool falling into traps and ultimately on his way to death (5:22, 22:5). If you hate it, you hate yourself (15:31). God disciplines his children out of love like any parent who cares about their future (3:12). If you are on the receiving end, listen humbly and don't lash out or be resentful. Be grateful for it, it's the proof you are His and He delights in you (3:11). Self-control and patience is more effective than power and force. Moderation is better than muscle (16:32).

Careful what you put into your brain and body. If you feed on wisdom, you'll become wiser. If you feed on trash, you'll get sick and/or become a fool (15:14).

Visiting people you like is always lovely, but don't visit too often or hang around too much. They'll hate you for it. (25:17).

Don't drink heavily or indulgently (23:20). If you drink too much, it feels like you've been bitten and poisoned by a viper (23:32). People who linger over alcohol and get a taste for it get suffering, sadness, arguments, complaints, needless bruises, and bloodshot eyes (23:29-30).

Eat good, healthy foods and enjoy their taste (24:13), but don't eat heavily or indulgently (23:20, 25:16). Gluttons end up poor because of the cost and constant drowsiness heavy foods like rich meats cause (23:21). Just as eating too much sugary goo can make you sick, probing too deeply into painful things can end up in you covered in dirt or dishonour (25:27). Once you're full, you won't want any more no matter how nice it is (27:7).

Lust is like fire. Keep it contained and be aware it can flame up and spread (6:25). Don't spend yourself emotionally and financially on women (31:3). Prostitutes will wreck any wealth or relationships you've built (29:3). Committing adultery will bring you ruin and death (2:18-19, 7:24-27, 9:14-17, 22:14). Enjoy the beauty and sexuality of your wife (5:15-19).

Don't gossip (11:13), slander (10:18), tattle (11:13), or lie (10:18). Gossip feels wonderful (11:13), like a tasty meal (18:8, 26:22) which goes right down well and smoothly (26:22). Don't do it.

Someone who boasts about giving gifts they never gave is like clouds and wind missing rain. They're empty and pointless. (25:14). Don't boast about tomorrow. You have no idea what it may bring (27:1).

Four things are never, ever satisfied in life: the grave, the empty womb, rainless land, and spreading fire. They never stop and never have enough (30:16).

Drinking

Beer and wine help relieve people's suffering, poverty, and misery. If you don't have those things, drinking has little purpose at all (31:6-7).

Wine makes you into a sarcastic cynic who looks down on people. Beer turns you into a common brawler. Either drink can lead you into conflict and trouble so it's best to stay away from them (20:1).

Drunkards end up poor because of the constant drowsiness alcohol causes (23:21).

Don't drink heavily or indulgently (23:20). If you drink too much, it feels like you've been bitten and poisoned by a viper (23:32).

People who linger over alcohol and get a taste for it get suffering, sadness, arguments, complaints, needless bruises, and bloodshot eyes (23:29-30).

You'll suffer hallucinations and confusing thoughts, and you'll be so numb to physical pain it will be like sleeping on the uncomfortable rigging of a ship in a storm wondering why you don't have an injury after being beaten (23:33-35).

You'll want to wake up from the stupor just so you can have another drink (23:35).

Leaders should not drink, in case they forget what they've

ruled or decided when under the influence. It could end in oppressed or poor people losing their rights (31:4-7).

Sexuality

Human sexuality is beautiful and powerful. It is a holy blessing from God designed to be the most intimate way two people can *know* each other; a binding force of sacred unity which draws the couple exclusively together as "one flesh".

Strength and vigour is the natural advantage of young men, which brings them glory. That includes women, who are attracted to it (20:29).

Lust is dangerous. It is evocatively described as playing with fire or hot coals; there is no safe way to handle it without severe consequences. You can't scoop fire into your lap without burning your clothes (6:27), as you can't walk on hot coals without scorching your feet (6:28). It grows like fire. It spreads like fire.

Women captivate you visually through your eyes (6:25) with their feminine mystique, such as coy glances, the clothing they use to capture your attention (7:10), as well as their breasts and graceful figure (5:19). Your eyes are never satisfied, always wanting more and more (27:20). But it doesn't matter how beautiful a woman is if she's crass or stupid. It's like a gold ring on a pig (11:22).

Seduction, allure, and enticement are also incited by smooth talk (2:16, 5:3, 6:24, 7:5, 7:21, 22:14).

Sexuality has a biological purpose, as does the response of men to female sexual behaviour. It is powerful in women because a barren or empty womb is never satisfied (30:16). They can be prone to abusing their mystique (7:9, 23:28).

A woman's natural beauty is inflammatory: it provokes and stirs up a man's lust on an inevitable and invariable basis. Don't let that happen. Be disciplined and self-controlled (6:25).

Men can spend themselves emotionally and financially on women. Don't. They can ruin leaders and powerful people (31:3). Spending money on prostitutes - the worst kind of wastage - will wreck any wealth or relationships you've built (29:3).

The similarity of male and female human sexuality to fire means there is only one safe place for it to exist appropriately and constructively (5:15-19). Your own wisdom on it will be like having a sister or relative with you at all times giving you great advice (7:4).

Adultery

An adulterant is something strange or poisonous which shouldn't be there. Within a marriage, it concerns the presence of another person - which *adulterates* the holy exclusivity defined in the covenant between a man and his wife.

Loyalty isn't common or typical to human beings. It's hard to find in either sex, so don't be surprised at its absence (20:6).

Predatory female adulterers target foolish young men drifting around with nothing to do (7:6-9), and will bring you to utter ruin and death (2:18-19, 7:24-27, 9:14-17, 22:14). They lie in wait like a criminal (23:28).

They are a crafty, predatory creatures who come out after dusk (7:9, 23:28) dressed in a staggeringly sexual way, like a prostitute (7:10). They claim to be searching for you, specifically (7:15). They are so brazen, they will physically grasp you and kiss you, even though you are a stranger (7:13, 22:14) in order to entice you to their house while their husband is allegedly away on a long journey for several weeks (7:19-20) to make love all night long (7:18). The temptation to go with such a person is a trap to lead you to your death in the slaughterhouse, similar to a snare an animal might get caught in (7:22-23, 22:14). Stay away from them at all costs and don't go near their house (5:8, 7:25). It's a matter of life and death

(2:18-19, 5:5, 7:27, 9:18).

There's nothing good which can come from being infatuated with anyone else other than your wife, such as a mistress, a prostitute, or a promiscuous woman (5:20). You can buy a prostitute for the same cost as a loaf of bread, but you won't get away with sleeping with another man's wife (6:26). You will get punished if you touch her (6:29), and it may get you killed (6:26).

The husband will be enraged with jealousy when he finds out (6:34). It doesn't matter how much money you or anyone else offers him as compensation, or just a bribe (6:35). He won't show you any mercy when he takes his revenge (6:34).

Nobody despises a thief who steals to survive, but they will still make him pay seven times what he stole or the cost of his own house to make amends (6:30-31). But if you sleep with someone else's wife, you are an idiot (6:32). You will only destroy yourself (6:32). You deserve the hatred and violence you receive (6:33), and the shame will never go away (6:34).

V

Relationships

Who you know, and how well you cooperate with them, is more important than what you know. Your life, and your own happiness, is determined by those closest to you.

Choosing Friends

Human behaviour is infectious. You will become like the people you spend time with. If you spend time with wise people, you will become wise. If you spend time with fools, you will become a fool and end up being harmed for it (13:20). If they're hot-tempered and instantly fly into a rage, you'll become the same and get into the same trouble they do. So don't have impulsive ragers as friends (22:24-25).

Guard your heart (4:23) and choose your friends carefully (12:26). Don't put your hope in men (11:7, 29:25). Everyone claims to be loyal and faithful, but it's genuinely hard to find people who genuinely are (20:6). Never forsake or abandon a friend, or a friend of your family (27:10); never withhold help if you can give it (3:27). Rescue people idiotically stumbling towards their own death and ruin (24:11).

The purpose of friendship is to share troubles with one another so the burden of them is lessened (17:17). The sign of true friendship is someone who always shows their love to you giving you an honest answer, in a gentle way (24:26).

The pleasantness of a friend comes from how they give you advice which comes from their heart, because of how they care about you (27:9). One person sharpens another in all ways, as you use iron to sharpen an iron sword (27:17). The hurt you feel from the blunt honesty a friend gives you is something you can trust because of their love for you and their good intentions. Your enemies will deceive you with kisses (27:6). A wise person loves those who rebuke them and becomes wiser for it (9:8-9).

True friends are a source of love and support in all weathers and all times. In really tough times, you need a friend who is more like a brother to you (17:17). You'll often have an amazing friend who is even closer than family (18:24).

Having unreliable fairweather friends you can't count on will bring you to ruin quicker than you think (18:24). Trusting or relying on unfaithful friends in times of trouble is like having a broken tooth or a lame foot. The pain distracts you all day and stops you from functioning (25:19). Don't trust your secrets with gossips because you will be betrayed (11:13).

Don't join, associate with, or ally with political rebels, troubles, or revolutionaries. God and the leaders they fight against will ruin them quickly in surprise attacks. You don't know how deep that trouble will go (24:21-22).

Don't accept a mean, resentful person's invite to dinner at their house. He'll tell you to eat and drink as much as you like, but secretly be counting the cost of them. When you realise, you'll vomit it back up and be angry you accepted the invite or were nice to him (23:6-8).

There are plenty of stupid things you can do to wreck your friendships. Don't become too over-familiar with other people's homes. Don't visit too often or hang around too much. They'll hate you for it. (25:17). If someone's sad, don't sing them lighthearted songs to try and cheer them up. It's like taking away their coat on a cold day, or pouring vinegar into their wounds (25:20). Wake or bless people loudly when it's early morning and they'll hate you for it no matter how good your intentions were (27:14).

If you want to grow closer to people, overlook the things they do which anger you the first time round. If they keep doing it, they'll end up pushing you away and separating (17:9). Friends are clumsy and often hurt you (18:24).

If a close friend is injured or offended, they are as unyielding as the stone walls of a military city in a terrible war (18:19). Love and faithfulness make amends for injuries (16:7), so speak to them in a soft, gentle voice (15:1).

The Girls To Avoid & Reject

The opposite traits of the girl you *do* want to marry are instructive to look out for as serious warning signs which define a woman as a poor candidate for a relationship. The deciding line is their *lack* of wisdom.

The first clue is her physical attendance: if she actually shows up where she is meant to be when she says she will. She should not be a lazy person who sleeps in or drifts without purpose (31:27). The same deficiency will be obvious in an inability or unwillingness to think ahead or plan sufficiently. She should not possess the chaotic or disorganised confusion which arises from being irresponsible (31:27).

The second major indicator is visual, in her appearance: a lack of taste in the way she presents herself, and dressing poorly in low-quality clothes if she can otherwise afford not to (31:22).

Thirdly, speaking carelessly and harshly, far too often (31:26), could be an indication she may be uncharitable and refuses to help others in need (31:20, 12:4); or even malevolent, often someone who tries to harm others, maybe you (31:12). If she constantly argues and quarrels, your married life is going to be utterly miserable (19:13, 27:15).

Fourth, study her capability and relationship with money.

She should not foolish with it, or useless at spotting opportunity (31:13-14, 32:24).

Lastly, avoid anyone who is untrustworthy and fickle (31:11), given to promiscuity or acute sexual behaviour (23:27-28), or isn't family-minded (31:28-29).

However, there is a particular type of woman you need to recognise and steer as far away as possible from. She has many names: the *Adulteress*, the *Seductress*, the *Temptress*, the *Forbidden Woman*, the *Immoral Woman*, the *Wayward Woman*, the *Promiscuous Woman* (7:5). Temptation, like Wisdom, is portrayed as female, because it is life-changing to young men.

Ancient Hebrew uses two words to describe her: *Zuwr*, which translates to "strange", "stranger", "estranged", "alienated", "strange woman" or "prostitute"; as well as *Nokriy*, which translates to "foreigner", "foreign woman", or "harlot".

This unusual root grammar describes a person who has forsaken, and subsequently become detached from, familiar social traditions such as the covenant of marriage to a husband, and ultimately, from God's ways. A non-Israelite racial alien neither Hebrew or destined to be separated as holy, whose worst nature is not constrained by her position as a wife and mother. An adulterant to food is an alien ingredient which adulterates it; a third person in a marriage adulterates the union of a covenant. It is a strange and foreign entity which is out of place and ruins what is clean and holy.

This type of person exists, and she is dangerous because of her recklessness and the wanton way she abuses the power of feminine mystique. She targets foolish young men drifting around with nothing to do, and will bring you to utter ruin and death (2:18-19, 7:24-27, 9:14-17, 22:14).

Recognise her by her sexual clothing (7:10), persuasive talk

(7:21), and the boldness of the way she lures you in (7:13). She's already ruined a lot of people before you (7:26, 23:28).

She is obviously defined by her mercurial nature and her treacherous character. She betrays. She is adulterous, double-minded, and perfidious (7:11). She appears and sounds highly appealing, but she's actually bitter and sharp (5:4). She is a trap, and the mouth she uses to charm you, and kiss you, is a huge pit in the ground people fall into to their death (23:27).

She talks in a seductive way (2:16, 7:5, 7:21). She knows what to say, and she's smooth (5:3, 6:24, 22:14).

She's been married before (2:17). She is usually separated, or her husband is away. She doesn't care about betraying him. (7:19-20). Often she's an ex-Christian, or pretending to still be one (2:17).

She is directionless and wanders without purpose, but she doesn't know it (5:6). Her wandering leads straight to your death and hers (5:5). She lies in wait like a criminal (23:28).

She is a crafty, predatory creature who comes out after dusk (7:9, 23:28) dressed in a staggeringly sexual way, like a prostitute (7:10). She wanders around different streets and corners (7:11-12), approaching foolish young men who are idling around without much apparent purpose (7:6-9) to stroke your ego by claiming she was searching for you, specifically (7:15). She is so brazen, she will physically grasp you and kiss you, even though you are a stranger (7:13, 22:14).

She will invite you to her house to commit adultery (9:15-17) while her husband is away on a long journey for several weeks (7:19-20), claiming she has immaculately prepared her perfectly soft and perfumed bedding (7:16-17) - a carnal sensory experience of colours and smells - in which to make love to her all night long (7:18). The temptation to go with her is a trap to lead you to your death in the slaughterhouse, similar to a snare an animal might get caught in (7:22-23, 22:14).

She refuses to concede she has done anything wrong. She eats haughtily, and takes pleasure in the evil she does (30:20). She doesn't know how unstable she is, doesn't think much about it, and doesn't particularly care (5:6, 9:13).

Stay away from her at all costs and don't go near her house (5:8, 7:25). It's a matter of life and death (2:18-19, 5:5, 7:27, 9:18).

If you do, you will lose your dignity and honour (5:9), and any wealth you have created will be lost to strangers who feast on it and use it to enrich themselves (5:10). If it happens to you, it's a clear sign of God's righteous anger over your lust and stupidity (22:14).

The Girl You Marry

It is exceptionally difficult to find a wife, and requires excluding many candidates. So difficult, in fact, almost every man finds it near impossible. A good wife is extremely rare and someone you should consider more valuable than the most precious jewel (31:10). She is the *exception*, rather than the rule. It will be the best investment, closest relationship, and most critical decision you ever make. She is such a blessing to a man she is like a royal crown on his head (12:4).

A wife is a wonderful and virtuous thing to have. She is a gift from God, and a sign of his affection and favour (18:22). If she's wise and prudent, you can trust she definitely came from God (19:14). It's good and holy you enjoy her so much you are romantically and sexually intoxicated by her (5:18-19).

The paragon of wives is known as *Noble* or *Excellent*, and often the *Virtuous Woman*. In Ancient Hebrew the word used is *Chayil*, which translates as "strength and valour". It indicates enormous warrior bravery and heroic courage in the face of terrible danger, which is derived from a steely strength of righteous character.

First, and above all, is you should choose her not on her temporary outward beauty, feminine mystique, or her flattering charm, but on the high quality of her *character*

(31:30).

She should be a Christian. And she should fear God (31:30).

She dresses immaculately in high-quality material, and appears extremely dignified (31:22), because she has the perfect taste of someone who is discriminating (31:13). She is physically strong, with muscular arms (31:17), which are open in approachable embrace to those less fortunate than her; whom she charitably gives money and help to generously (31:20). Her kindheartedness is the source of her honour (11:16).

She is an early riser; a morning person; someone who gets up before everyone else to care for them (31:15). Yet she also works extremely hard deep into the night (31:17-18) and stubbornly refuses to be lazy (31:27).

She speaks carefully (31:26), showing her diplomatic wisdom, and her prudence in avoiding the folly of gossip, slander, and inflammatory coarseness. She gives good advice and instructions in a kind way (31:26), but also laughs heartily and doesn't worry or fret too much about the anxiety tomorrow will bring (31:25).

She is chaste and sexually moderate (23:27-28).

She cares about you and does what is best for you; in your best interests. She doesn't try to harm you verbally, emotionally, or physically. She always brings you kindness and care with a positive and warm smile (31:12). Her humble and contrite spirit doesn't burden others' lives with constant arguing and quarreling (19:13, 27:15).

She is creative and enterprising. What she doesn't need, she sells for a profit (31:13-14, 32:24). She is a financially shrewd investor who can spot opportunity and make a healthy profit (31:16).

She is trustworthy. You find it easy to trust her. She is highly competent, reliable, and does what she says she will. Her defining characteristic is how *capable* she is (31:11).

She is extremely diligent and conscientious. She observes every detail (31:27), which gives her the immense skill of providing things your home needs. She is a faultless provider (31:22-24) who sets out schedules for her children and staff (31:15, 31:27) which shows in the way they effortlessly like, respect, and obey her (31:28-29).

Her work is worthy of praise from *everyone*, not just her family. She should be honoured, because she deserves it (31:31).

Marriage

Men feel loneliness extremely intensely. It's good to be married. Marriage was ordained by God (Gen 2:23–24) to symbolically reflect the relationship between Him, the bridegroom, and the Church, His bride, to help us understand it.

Marry in haste as early as possible, and repent at leisure.

The wrong wife is a catastrophic decision lasting a lifetime. A cold, mean-hearted wife is such a burden it feels like decay in your own bones (12:4).

A contemptible woman, i.e. a prostitute, who manages to marry is a disaster (30:23). But equally, an adulterous or sexually promiscuous wife will get you into deep trouble fast. She's like a small, narrow well you trip and fall down into which is hard to see. She's predatory and waits for men to corrupt (23:27-28).

A wife who constantly argues and quarrels is exhausting and feels like the water-drip torture of a roof endlessly leaking on your head (19:13, 27:15). You'll be better off living somewhere as inhospitable as the desert (21:19), or on the far corner of the roof of your house than share the building with her (21:9, 25:24). Restraining her is impossible; it's like trying to grasp liquid in your hand or holding back the wind (27:16).

A good wife is a wonderful and virtuous thing to have. She is from God, and a sign of his affection and favour (18:22). If she's wise and prudent, you can trust she definitely came from God (19:14). A Godly wife is such a blessing to a man it is like a crown on his head (12:4). She deserves to be honoured (31:31).

Stick faithfully to your wife, and her alone. Rejoice in her (5:15, 5:18). Enjoy her breasts (5:19), as well as her graceful figure, and lovingkindness (5:19). Enjoy being intoxicated with her sexually and emotionally (5:19). She is not to be shared with others and you are not to share yourself either (5:16-17).

Home & Family

Home's where you belong. People who flee it are like a bird fleeing their own nest (27:8). It's a wise thing to build your home (14:1). Homes are built and furnished through wisdom (24:3-4). Children love to be proud of who their parents are (17:6), and grandchildren are a prize and a royal crown to grandparents (17:6).

The houses of Godly people are blessed by God (3:33, 15:6) and He ensures they are immunised from disaster (12:7).

Borders, fences, walls, and boundaries were put there for a reason by the people who came before you. Don't move them or tear them down unless you know why they were put there in the first place (22:28, 23:10). Be careful of what you develop or refurnish because it could be providing something for the poor. Doing something to it might do them an injustice (13:23).

Your wife is ultimately who makes and runs your home because she comes from God (19:14) and deserves to be honoured for what she brings to you (31:31). She watches over everything and everyone diligently from before dawn until late (31:15, 31:27); she supervises and grows the children, who love and respect her (31:28); she provides all bedding and furnishings far in advance (31:21-22); and what is not needed, she uses to sell and invest (31:16-18, 31:24).

It's a good thing to get on with your neighbours. Don't despise the people who live nearby you (14:21). Don't lie about them (25:17) or plot against other people who live nearby and trust you (3:29). If disaster strikes and you have a choice between seeking refuge between a relative far away and your neighbour, go to your neighbour. Don't take long trips when you're in trouble (27:10).

However, if your neighbour is flattering you, it's almost certainly because he's softening you up because he's up to no good (29:5). Don't visit too often or hang around too much. They'll hate you for it. (25:17).

Wake or bless people loudly when it's early morning and they'll hate you for it no matter how good your intentions were (27:14).

The happiness of your home can make or break your life and it will show up publicly (21:8). It's better to have a small serving of food made with love than a huge feast created alongside hatred and resentment (15:17). It's better to have unappetizing dry bread in peace and quiet than hours of feasting in a house where everyone is quarreling (17:1). The source of difficulty is marrying the wrong woman (19:13, 27:15).

Love and faithfulness make amends for injuries (16:7), so speak in a soft, gentle voice (15:1).

Parenting & Children

All children are born foolish and without any knowledge of the world (22:15). Who they are is set in their early years. What you indoctrinate them in when they are small will be who they are as an adult. They won't change, even when they are old themselves. (22:6). Children love to be proud of who their parents are (17:6)

Children aren't a special case. They are little humans who gain a reputation for their behaviour, like anyone else. And they don't always have good motives, or behave morally (20:11). Harsh, loving discipline applied consistently erodes their inherent foolishness away over time and builds wisdom (22:15).

God disciplines his children out of love like any parent who cares about their future (3:12). If you are on the receiving end, listen humbly and don't lash out or be resentful. Be grateful for it, it's the proof you are His and He delights in you (3:11).

Discipline produces hope (19:18). Wisdom is embedded into children by discipline and punishment. Warnings, rebukes, reprimands, and stern caretaking is what transforms them from foolishness to individuals of character (29:15). If you discipline them, they will delight you and give you peace (29:17). Severe discipline and punishment drives out evil from the inside (20:30).

If you love your children, you must discipline them as a matter of their life and death. If you spare them, you're not helping. It's actually hatred for them. A refusal to correct is a refusal to love and contributing to their death. (13:24, 19:18, 23:14). Don't hold back when you apply discipline and apply it as harshly as necessary because it won't kill them (23:13); on the contrary, it will save them from death (23:14).

A father's purpose is to use his authority responsibly to instruct and command his children. You should listen. If you do, it will be like royal garments and jewelry you wear throughout your life. (1:7-8). Listen to your father and always give him your full attention because he wants the best for you (23:26).

A mother's purpose is to teach her children. You should not abandon or give up listening to her. (1:7), even when she is older and doesn't play a significant role in your life anymore (23:22). A mother should be joyful, just as a father is (23:25).

A wise child who follows instruction (13:1, 23:22) brings his father joy (10:1, 15:20, 23:15-16, 23:24) and lets him dismiss critics with contempt (27:11). Gathering crops in advance is an example of a prudent son (10:5). It's a mark of prudence to follow correction (15:5) and his father's joy will continue into adulthood if he comes to love wisdom (29:3). He will grow into someone who chooses his friends wisely (28:7).

Listen to your parents. Don't bother praying desperately to God for help if you can't even follow the basic instructions they have given you (28:9).

It's utterly miserable to have a foolish child. There's no joy in it at all (17:21). It's the mark of a fool to reject parents' discipline (15:5). If he's a fool, it brings a father deep grief

(17:25) and ruin (19:13). Laziness and sleeping in during harvest time is an example of a disgraceful son (10:5). A foolish child who ignores his mother's teaching is embarrassed and disgraced by a child who has been left undisciplined (29:15). They bring her grief and bitterness (10:1, 12:21, 17:25), and as an adult, it's clear they stupidly hate her (15:20). They may choose to associate with fat greedy people, who bring shame and disgrace (28:7).

A child who severely mistreats their parents, such as stealing from them or driving them away by force, is a disgrace (19:26, 28:24). If you bring disgrace on your family that way, or by abuse or exploitation, you won't receive any inheritance and will end up in you working for smarter people (11:29). Just cursing them will end up in you losing the ability to find direction and the right way to go in life (20:20, 30:17). You are a partner and friend of criminals (28:24).

Parents leave their houses and fortune to their children to pass on generational wealth (19:14). A wise employee will be given part of childrens' inheritance as one of the family, particularly if there's a bad child they end up in charge of and favoured ahead of (17:2). If an inheritance is claimed too soon, even just early, it won't end up in increased prosperity over the long term (20:21).

Grandchildren are a prize, and a royal crown to grandparents (17:6).

VI

Prospering

*Getting ahead isn't a mystery at all. It takes
diligence, discipline, faithfulness, and is the product
of a righteous life pursuing wisdom.*

The Art Of Success

God protects and rewards people who do their best to live well and be free of blame (2:7-8). He pays special attention to people who are loyal to Him (2:8), and He has the final say in anything you do (16:33). Don't put your hope in men (11:7, 29:25) or trust in yourself, it's foolish (28:26). Don't try to figure things out on your own. Refer to God and trust Him. Agree with Him (3:5-6). His way is a refuge (10:29). Before all else, tell Him even the smallest of your plans and ask Him to bless them, so He can agree and establish the successful end result (16:3).

You should do all you can possibly do in your own capacity to succeed. Prepare everything as diligently as you are able to in the greatest detail. But ultimately, the end result, the decision of victory or loss is up to God. Control over the whole situation and victory itself belongs to Him (21:31). He sees everything you do at all times and scrutinises it (5:21).

Complex things like houses are only built through wisdom. They only exist because of wisdom (24:23). Wisdom is more important than strength, and intelligence is far more powerful than anything else (24:5). Delight in it rather than human scheming (10:23). Discipline is what will save you, or keep you from falling into traps and death (5:22, 22:5). If you hate it, you hate yourself (15:31).

Success is a result of understanding the importance of disciplining yourself (10:17) and valuing correction (15:5), as well as storing up wisdom and knowledge over time (10:14). If you take in correction, you'll grow smarter, and be at home with wise people; counted as one of them (15:31). Self-control and patience is more effective than power and force. Moderation is better than muscle (16:32). The difference between wise people and fools is their attitude towards discipline and correction. If you're wise, you'll love and value both. A fool hates them (12:1). A rebuke you give to a wise person is welcomed (9:8-9) and goes in deeper than a hundred lashes goes into a fool (17:10).

Smart people *act*, and don't just keep their wisdom in their head (13:16). Hard work generates profit (14:23) and rewards (12:14). Wanting something intensely but lacking the wisdom to get it won't get you anywhere. You'll simply miss the target faster than if you didn't care (19:2). If you guard your labour and investment diligently, you will get to enjoy it in its fullness after it has grown (27:18).

Stay focused and keep your eyes on the wise course of action (17:24). Smart planning done patiently, and diligently, generates profit, whereas running into things quickly bankrupts you (21:5). Keep your own counsel and your cards close to your chest. Don't boast or over-share. (12:23). Be careful of what you develop or refurnish because it could be an injustice against the poor (13:23).

Careful what you put into your brain and body. If you feed on wisdom, you'll become wiser. If you feed on trash, you'll get sick and/or become a fool (15:14).

The praise or admonition you receive will be in proportion

to how prudent others recognise you to be (12:8). A good reputation and receiving good will comes from being dedicated to being loving and faithful. (3:4) It is so important you should permanently install those things in your heart, and wear them like royal dressings (3:3, 4:9, 6:21).

How do you work out what to do and make plans? Get advice. Lots of it. (20:18). You can secure victory by getting truthful counsel from a lot of different advisors. The more opinions you get, the more likely you are to succeed (11:14, 15:22, 20:18, 24:6). If you don't get counsel or advice, you'll fail (15:22). Wise people listen to advice (12:15, 13:10).

Choose your friends carefully (12:26) because behaviour is infectious (13:20). Guard your heart vigilantly because everything in your life flows from it (4:23).

Your prosperity will increase directly in line with your generosity (11:25, 22:9) and how willing you are to accept instruction (16:20). The more you give, the more you will get back (11:24). If you refresh others, they will reciprocate and refresh you when you need it (11:25). If you give to the poor, you'll never lack anything, but if you turn a blind eye to them, you'll suffer curse after curse (28:27). People will pray that God blesses you if you are willing to sell or share food you can spare (11:26, 22:9). Sowing goodness and mercy reaps a great reward (11:18, 11:27).

Humble people receive honour for their character and things they achieve. As pride precedes and provokes ruin, the opposite is also true: humility precedes and provokes honour. People pour honour on those who are humble about their success and lowly in spirit (15:33, 18:12, 29:23), and those who loyally defend whom they serve (27:18). Never praise yourself. Let an outsider do it for you (27:2).

There are things God detests, so avoid them (6:16): having an arrogant attitude, lying, harming the innocent (6:17), evil scheming, running to do evil (6:18), providing false witness testimony, and stirring up trouble socially (6:19). Sin doesn't discriminate. It condemns anyone and everyone, and even entire countries (14:34). You won't prosper if your motives are bad, and they come from the heart (17:20). Your own duplicity, caused by the snare of your own evil desires, are what caused your troubles (11:3, 11:6, 12:8). Death and destruction are never, ever satisfied. They always want more and more company (27:20).

Most of the time it's your own stupidity which leads to your ruin. Take responsibility. It's not God's fault you screwed up. You have no case against Him and no right to be angry with Him (19:3). Did your eyes wander everywhere (17:24)? What's the point of praying to God for help when you won't follow the simple instructions of your parents and friends? Your prayers are detestable (28:9).

Rules and commands are there for a reason. Follow them, and you'll be OK. Ignore them to live recklessly, and it will end up with you dying (19:16). Having the wrong friends means you pick up traits which bring ruin (10:17).

God can and will fix mistakes, so forget your ideas and trust completely in Him (3:5-6). He will stop you from being snared in traps (3:26). He disciplines his children out of love like any parent who cares about their future (3:12). If you are on the receiving end, listen humbly and don't lash out or be resentful. Be grateful for it, it's the proof you are His and He delights in you (3:11).

Don't try to deceive God or deny what you know. He guards your life and can see everything. He'll pay you back exactly for what you've done (24:12). Hardening your heart, or turning against Him, will send you down the wrong road land you in trouble (28:14). Covering up your sins and errors won't end up in you prospering from it. Confess and renounce them and you'll find forgiveness and mercy (28:13).

If you don't listen, you'll be furious with yourself in your last days for rejecting discipline, disobeying teachers, ignoring instructors, and refusing to accept being corrected (5:12). You'll stray and end up in a bad way (19:27). If you're still stubborn after dozens of collapses and rebukes, there will come a day when your life simply falls apart, seemingly by surprise, and can't be repaired. There's an endpoint to the mistakes (29:1). Even whole nations collapse because they have no guidance. Without good leadership and direction, entire countries fall to pieces (11:14).

There are simple, obvious things you can do to avoid ruin. Shun and avoid evil people (2:22, 10:30, 11:20, 12:7, 14:11, 17:11). If you see danger, hide, run, avoid, or get away from it. Find refuge (22:3, 27:12).

Don't take bribes (15:27). Don't get trapped in vows from taking them lightly or impulsively (20:25). Don't withhold food (11:26). Don't give gifts to the rich (22:16). Don't trust your secrets with gossips because you will be betrayed (11:13).

Don't hang around the lives of Godly people trying to exploit them, intervene in their affairs, or burglarize their home. (24:15). Don't join, associate with, or ally with political rebels, troubles, or revolutionaries. God and the leaders they fight against will ruin them quickly in surprise attacks. You don't know how deep that trouble will go (24:21-22).

If you're impulsive, explosive, or otherwise lack self-control, you're as vulnerable as a strong fortress citadel whose walls have been broken through. Your defenses are down and you will be routed by people looking to overcome you (25:28). Don't respond impulsively when someone irritates you or insults you. Wait. Then overlook it (12:16, 19:11).

Big leaps or boasts of pride or haughtiness are always followed by disgrace (11:2, 16:18, 29:23). God will tear down the source of your pride (15:25).

Business & The Workplace

Business must always be honest and be of the utmost integrity. Scales and measures must be just, fair, and accurate under all circumstances because God is Holy (11:1, 16:11, 20:10). Hard work generates profit (14:23) and rewards (12:14). Smart planning done patiently, and diligently, generates profit, whereas running into things quickly bankrupts you (21:5). If you guard your labour and investment diligently, you will get to enjoy it in its fullness after it has grown (27:18).

Whenever you make money or produce a harvest, give the first and best piece to God to honour Him (3:9). The more you do that, the larger your accumulated profits and subsequent harvests will become (3:10).

A good name is worth more than gold or silver, and it'll help you to re-earn both if you come to ruin (22:1). A good reputation and goodwill comes from being dedicated to being loving and faithful (3:4). If you gain a reputation for good judgment, you'll win favour and luxury (13:15).

Your boss's attitude towards you will be based on your character and behaviour. If you act wisely, they will love you and delight in you. If you're foolish and act shamefully, their anger will get worse and worse over time, emerging eventually as fury (14:35).

Don't slander a loyal worker or good employee to their boss. They'll condemn you and punish you for it. (30:10). If you protect your boss, you'll receive honour (27:18).

Hungry people work hard. Their hunger drives them on and isn't a bad thing because it earns them more wages. If you're full of food, you're sleepy. (16:26). You can't keep workers, employees, or staff in line with tough talk. You need more. They'll listen and understand, but they won't respond or change (29:19). If you pamper them and pander to them from the beginning, they'll end up disobedient and disrespectful (29:21).

Make sure you have high quality equipment for producing what you plan to. If not, you won't have a harvest (14:4). Always know the exact condition of your investments, accounts, and resources, at all times. Give them extremely careful attention in great detail. Then you will have all the things your family and employees need (27:23-27).

Do things in logical, practical ordered steps which make sense. Priorities and dependencies. First deal with the work which provides the harvest of your income and means. Then build what you want. Only start on your house after you have planted your fields first (24:27). It's better to be an ordinary small businessman with a small number of employees than to act important when you don't have money to eat. Don't fake it to make it (12:9, 13:7).

Sowing goodness and mercy reaps a great reward (11:18). The more you give, the more you will get back (11:24). Your prosperity will increase directly in line with your generosity (11:25, 22:9) and how willing you are to accept instruction (16:20). If you refresh others, they will reciprocate and refresh you when you need it (11:25). If you give to the poor, you'll never lack anything, but if you turn a blind eye to them, you'll suffer curse after curse (28:27). People will pray that God blesses you if you are willing to sell or share food you can spare (11:26, 22:9).

Leaders always want the best of everything; the best quality and workmanship, the best materials, and the most diligent suppliers. If you're skillful in what you do, leaders will seek you out and poach you to work exclusively for them (22:29).

If you want to get an appointment with someone powerful, giving them a gift will open the door (18:16). If you want them to be friends with you, speak gracefully and make clear your love of good people with pure motives (22:11).

When you have dinner with a powerful person, the food is a trap. Don't stare in awe, and don't eat much. If you're hungry or a glutton, put a knife to your throat to stop yourself if you have to. Your appetite and manners are being watched (23:1-3). Don't exalt yourself or honour yourself. Don't claim a place in his inner circle. Both of those things will end up in him humiliating you in front of them. Wait for him to invite you or call for you (25:6-7). If you want to persuade them, you need to employ patience. It will only happen that way. Speak gently. It's more powerful than you think. (25:15).

Choose middlemen who relay messages for you carefully. An evil will bring trouble, and but one you can trust heals the situation (13:17). Using a fool is so perilous it's like cutting off your own feet or drinking poison (26:6). Light in their eyes will bring happiness and joy to the recipient (15:30). Their trustworthiness and integrity refreshes the sender's spirit like a cold drink of snow water in the heat of harvest (25:13).

If you are slack in your work, you let down your friends and colleagues. It's destructive to others and like a form of vandalism (18:7). Sleeping when it is time to work is disgraceful (10:5). Don't hire lazy people. They are so obnoxious to employers they are like the taste of raw vinegar, or smoke in the eyes (10:26). If you hire a fool, they will injure everyone around them like an archer shooting and wounding at random (26:10).

Customers complain bitterly so they can drive down the price. Once they've got their discount, they run home to boast about it (20:14).

To prevent people from jockeying for position or disagreeing about their rank and position, roll the dice randomly to smooth things over and keep powerful rivals calm (18:18).

Don't offer bribes. Offering a bribe to someone feels good. Like a magic spell or a faultless plan which can never fail (17:8). Don't take bribes. It'll cost you your life (15:27).

Wealth & Riches

Get your priorities straight. It's good to leave an inheritance for your grandchildren as well as your children (13:22), but wisdom is far more precious than any kind of material worth. It's far better to be wise than to be rich (3:13-15). Don't exhaust yourself trying to get rich or rely on your own cleverness (23:4). If you put your trust in wealth instead of God, or you're eager to run after money, you will fall and come to ruin (11:28, 28:20). Don't be naive or under any kind of illusion: wealth and riches bring more trouble with them than their benefits (15:16).

Wealth is fleeting. It disappears in a second. Riches can be so temporary they seem to grow wings and fly off the moment you glance at them (23:5). Wealth does not endure, and your great grandchildren aren't guaranteed what you pass to them (27:24).

It's better to have a good reputation and be well thought of than to be rich. A good name is worth more than gold or silver, and it'll help you to re-earn both if you come to ruin (22:1). A good reputation and goodwill comes from being dedicated to being loving and faithful (3:4).

Riches are a gift from wisdom which she carries in her hands, along with a long life (3:16). Riches and honour which don't disappear are a long-term by-product and fruit of wisdom itself (8:18), and she fills treasuries with inheritance (8:21). It rests as a crown on wise people to identify them, and generates more and more returns and profits (14:24). You can't buy it. If you're a fool, you're not going to be able to understand it either (17:16), and you're totally out of place with its benefits (19:10).

Focus on these things above money, as they give you the means to earn it: fearing God (10:22), wisdom (3:13-15), and your reputation (22:1). Invest in truth, wisdom, instruction, and insight and do not sell even a piece of them (23:23). They are what fill the rooms of your house with expensive treasures (24:4).

Earned wealth comes from God (10:22), but ruthless men can build it too despite being dishonourable (11:16). If it isn't inherited directly through parents as cash and property (19:14), it is built *slowly, growing little by little, over a long time* (13:11).

There's no secret here: if you chase pipe dreams, you'll get nothing. If you put the physical labour in, you'll have plenty to eat (12:11, 28:19). If all you do is talk, you'll end up in poverty with nothing (14:23, 28:19). Hard work generates profit (14:23) and rewards (12:14). Bad work gets paid with a bad check; good work gets solid pay (11:18).

The difference between poverty and wealth is the faithful diligence you put into your work consistently over time. Diligence brings wealth (10:6, 28:20) and luxurious living (12:27) which fully satisfies (13:4). If you guard your labour and investment diligently, you will get to enjoy it in its fullness after it has grown (27:18). It will take you to the top of the pile (12:24), and the powerful people will seek you out to contract you exclusively because you're the best at what you do (22:29). The praise or admonition you receive will be in proportion to how prudent others recognise you to be (12:8).

Make sure you have high quality equipment for producing what you plan to. If not, you won't have a harvest (14:4). Always know the exact condition of your investments, accounts, and resources, at all times. Give them extremely careful attention in great detail. Then you will have all the things your family and employees need (27:23-27). Knowing your calendar and strategy is crucial. Gathering crops in summer ahead of winter time is a smart thing to do (10:5, 21:20). Smart planning done patiently, and diligently, generates profit, whereas running into things quickly bankrupts you (21:5)

Your ability to work hard and generate money is correlated to sleep. If you sleep too much you'll miss a lot of the day and be drowsy through it. It'll make you poor, quickly. Stay awake and work hard and you'll generate more than you need (20:13).

Stingy, mean, tight people always want to get rich. They think their stinginess is the secret to accruing money, when it's the opposite. Their destiny is to be poor and live in ruin (28:22). The more you give, the more you will get back (11:24); your prosperity will increase directly in line with your generosity (11:25, 22:9) and how willing you are to accept instruction (16:20). If you refresh others, they will reciprocate and refresh you when you need it (11:25).

It's better to be an ordinary small businessman with a small number of employees than to act important when you don't have money to eat. Don't fake it to make it (12:9, 13:7). Don't spend money giving wealthy people gifts which they don't want or need, because you'll end up ruined and poor (22:16)

Whenever you make money or produce a harvest, give the first and best piece to God to honour Him (3:9). The more you do that, the larger your accumulated profits and subsequent harvests will become (3:10). God blesses the home of those who try to live rightly (3:33) and protects them from going hungry (10:3). His blessing arrives without requiring you to have worked hard for it (10:22).

Wealth brings problems. It's better to be poor and fear God, than to be extremely rich and have all the extreme trouble that accompanies it (15:16).

Rich people deceive and delude themselves in a circular way: because they have wealth, they are convinced it is evidence of their own wisdom and virtue. A poor person who is wise can see right through the illusion (28:11). Once you have some wealth, you'll wrongly come to think of it as a fortress or a fortified city nobody can overcome, where you're safe (10:15, 18:11).

Money attracts people to you. You can be sure you'll have a lot of friends (14:20, 19:4); everyone wants to be friends with the rich because of the freebies it means they can benefit from (11:6). Social leeches and freeloaders only produce two things: a demand to be given things for free immediately, and another cry for exactly the same (30:15). And riches make you vulnerable to being held hostage through lawsuits and extortion which are like a ransom on your life (13:8). Appearances can be deceiving: rich people often dress down to avoid attention so you never know who you could be talking to (13:7).

If you become obsessed with pleasure, like heavy drinking and expensive fine foods, you're never going to build riches or be satisfied. You'll spend all the money you earn on them instead of stockpiling your revenues (21:17). If you spend time and money on prostitutes, you'll destroy everything you've built by squandering it (29:3). The wise route is to store luxury goods up instead of consuming them impulsively (21:20).

Rich people rule over the poor. It's just how life is (22:7). Wealth can cause you to speak harshly and unsympathetically to poor people who often beg you for mercy (18:23). Everyone deserts you when you're poor, and it can definitely happen to you too (19:4). Wealth is useless when you have to face God's judgment (11:4) alongside poor people when He made you both. You have that in common (22:2).

If you make your money by profiting from exploiting the poor or charging them interest, all you are doing is collecting the money for God to inevitably give to someone else who loves Him and deserves it more (28:8). Be careful of what you develop or refurnish because it could be providing something for the poor. Doing something to it might do them an injustice (13:23). If you oppress the poor to increase your wealth, you'll come to ruin and poverty (22:16) because God is their defender of their fields (23:10-11).

Be careful: God loves the poor, they are special to Him, and dismissing them will guarantee His wrath (14:31, 17:5). Be kind to them and you'll be blessed and marked out as a Godly person (14:21, 19:17) who lacks nothing (28:27). If you do, you're honouring God (14:31) and lending to Him (19:17). Fear God. If you think your riches make you powerful, just you wait and see how wealthy He is and the power He has (1:7, 2:5).

Riches you get from fraud or criminality have no value (10:2), will drain away (13:11), and be stored for transfer to good people who live in a Godly way (13:22). If you get greedy, or take bribes, you and your family will end up being ruined (15:27). If you made your money by lying, it's a deadly trap and your illicit rewards will evaporate like vapour (21:5). The money looks and tastes wonderful initially, but quickly turns to gravel in your mouth (20:17). You cannot become established through those kind of riches (12:3). It's better to be the lowest of the low with the poorest people than share in stolen goods with arrogant criminals (16:19). It's better to have a little as a Godly person than make a lot of money unjustly (16:8, 28:6).

Financial Debt

Don't be under any illusions: debt is slavery. People who borrow money are enslaved to those who lend it to them. That's how the relationship between them works (22:7)..

Don't underwrite a debt security for any stranger outside your family (11:15, 17:18, 22:26), because it's a trap you've fallen into created by your own mouth (6:1-2). If they can't pay, you could lose your own home, or the bed underneath you which you sleep on (22:26-27).

If you have, get out of it immediately. Get out of it right now, and don't stop begging to get out until you are exhausted. Don't sleep, and don't stop until you've exhausted the person you've promised it to so much they release you from it (6:3-5). You'll stay safe if you refuse to shake hands on a deal like that (11:15, 17:18).

If someone you don't know puts up collateral for a stranger, get a deposit. They're going to lose it (20:16, 27:13).

Poverty & Ruin

The rich rule over the poor (22:7). Poverty is a curse which to the poor and destroys them (10:15). You might be born into it, or earn it through your own behaviour (19:3). God made us all regardless of our material worth (22:2).

It's better to have nothing and fear God, than to be filthy rich and unable to sleep at night (15:16), speak in a vile way (19:1, 19:22), or be evil (37:16). Poor people can see through the self-delusion of the rich (28:11). It's better to be poor and honest than rich and crooked (28:6).

Poor people are ignored and shunned by everyone, even by their closest friends, relatives, and the people who live next to them which they plead to for help (14:20, 19:4, 19:7). Poor people live as prey among hungry predators wanting to hunt and devour them (30:14). Wealth can cause you to speak harshly and unsympathetically to poor people who often beg you for mercy (18:23). They beg the rich for mercy and are treated harshly (18:23). When you're hungry, even bitter foods taste sweet like honey (27:7).

Do not exploit the poor because they are poor (22:22). If you make your money by profiting from exploiting the poor or charging them interest, all you are doing is collecting the money for God to inevitably give to someone else who loves

Him and deserves it more (28:8). If you oppress the poor to increase your wealth, you'll come to ruin and poverty (22:16) because God is their defender (23:10-11).

God made both rich and poor and helped them perceive (29:13) and you'll face God's judgment together equally (11:4, 22:2). If you close your ears to their cries, you'll be ignored by God in return (21:13) and it'll be like receiving curse after curse (28:27). If you're cruel to them or gloat over their suffering, you're insulting God, who made them and loves them. Be careful: God loves the poor, they are special to Him, and dismissing them will guarantee His wrath (14:31, 17:5).

Be kind to them and you'll be blessed and marked out as a Godly person (14:21, 19:17) who lacks nothing (28:27). If you do, you're honouring God (14:31) and lending to Him (19:17). Speak up for them and defend their rights (31:8-9). A leader who gives them justice fairly will see his name immortalised in history (29:14).

Your own stupidity can lead to your ruin. Take responsibility. It's not God's fault you screwed up. You have no case against Him and no right to be angry with Him (19:3, 19:27). If you're still stubborn after dozens of collapses and rebukes, there will come a day when your life simply falls apart, seemingly by surprise, and can't be repaired. There's an endpoint to the mistakes. (29:1).

As there are things you can do to ensure wealth, there are things you can do to ensure poverty and ruin:h

- Being evil, seeking evil, loving evil, or doing evil (2:22, 10:30, 11:20, 12:7, 14:11, 17:11)
- Committing adultery (2:18-19, 5:5, 7:27, 9:18).
- Sleeping too much (6:9-11)

- Lust (6:27-28)
- Laziness (10:4, 20:13)
- Not being diligent in your work (10:6)
- Foolish chattering (10:10)
- Duplicity (11:3)
- Lacking guidance (11:14)
- Lying (11:5, 11:9)
- Cruelty (11:17)
- Withholding what you are able to give (11:24, 11:26)
- Putting your trust in riches instead of God (11:28)
- Opening your mouth and not guarding it (13:3)
- Bad faith (13:15)
- Ignoring instruction (13:18)
- Talking instead of doing (14:23)
- Not getting advice and counsel (15:22)
- Taking bribes (15:27)
- Pride (15:33, 18:12, 29:23)
- Offering bribes (17:8)
- Soliciting conflict (17:19)
- Having lots of fairweather friends, but no real ones (18:24)
- Having foolish children (19:13)
- Living recklessly (19:16)
- Giving false testimony (19:5, 19:9)
- Angering a leader (20:2, 16:14)
- Cursing your parents or criminally victimising them (20:20, 30:17)
- Hastily and impulsively running into things without thinking them through (21:5)
- Speaking rashly (21:23)
- Loving pleasures like alcohol and fine foods (21:17)
- Not fleeing from danger (22:3, 27:12)

- Sowing injustice (22:8)
- Oppressing poor people (22:16)
- Giving gifts to the rich (22:16)
- Drunkenness and alcoholism (23:21)
- Securing a stranger's debt (22:26-27)
- Joining troublemakers and revolutionaries (24:21-22)
- Honouring yourself when in powerful company (25:6-7)
- Lacking self-control (25:28)
- Being deceived by flattery (26:28)
- Being miserly or stingy (28:22)
- Ignoring the cries of the poor (28:27)
- Spending money on prostitutes (29:3)

Hacks & Workarounds

If in doubt, shut up (10:19, 11:12, 30:32) and listen (18:13). Keep your cards close to your chest (12:23). You'll appear thoughtful (17:28).

Never praise yourself. Let an outsider do it for you (27:2).

Be suspicious of anyone flattering you. They're setting you up (29:5). If you see danger, hide, run, avoid, or get away from it. Find refuge (22:3, 27:12).

How do you work out what to do and make plans? Get advice. Lots of it from lots of different people (20:18).

To calm someone down who is angry, speak in a soft, gentle voice (15:1), and give them a gift in secret; preferably financial in nature (21:14).

If multiple warring parties can't agree, roll a dice and use randomness for allocation and priorities to soothe the friction (18:18).

If there is conflict, quarreling, and strife, find divisive stirrers and gossipers, then expel them mercilessly (22:10).

Don't hire lazy people (10:26) or fools (26:10).

Protect your boss, you'll receive honour (27:18).

Don't slander a loyal worker or good employee to their boss. They'll condemn you and punish you for it (30:10).

If someone you don't know puts up collateral for a stranger, get a deposit. They're going to lose it (20:16, 27:13).

Don't take vows lightly or impulsively. You'll get trapped in them not having thought things through (20:25).

If disaster strikes and you have a choice between seeking refuge between a relative far away and your neighbour, go to your neighbour. Don't take long trips when you're in trouble (27:10).

If you want to get an appointment with someone powerful, give them a gift (18:16). Once you're in, don't fall in love with the lavish foods or eat much of them (23:1-3). Don't honour yourself, and wait to be called on (25:6-7). Then speak gracefully and gently (25:15), making clear your love of good people with pure motives (22:11).

Do things in logical, practical ordered steps which make sense. Priorities and dependencies. First deal with the work which provides the harvest of your income and means. Then build what you want. Only start on your house after you have planted your fields first (24:27).

Whenever you make money or produce a harvest, give the first and best piece to God to honour Him (3:9).

If you're rich, dress down to avoid attention (13:7).

Remove corrupt officials and managers underneath you to protect your own position (20:28, 25:5).

Confess and renounce your sins and errors and you'll find forgiveness and mercy. Don't attempt cover-ups (28:13).

To determine someone's guilt or innocence regarding a specific situation, look at their ordinary life more broadly. Their character will be displayed in their background and everyday dealings (21:8).

VII

Governing

The most prosperous among us inherit a position where they are required to use their wisdom for more than merely their own life, and intervene on behalf of others.

Justice

Justice comes from God (29:26), and judgments should be fair. Speak up for people who don't have a voice or are destitute (31:8-9). He hates the condemnation of the innocent (17:15), false testimony (6:18), and the acquittal of the guilty (17:15). A correct ruling court is wonderful. It's like apples made of gold, embedded in silver (25:11).

Rules and commands are there for a reason. Follow them, and you'll be OK. Ignore them to live recklessly, and it will end up with you dying (19:16). Don't take vows lightly or impulsively (20:24). Don't take bribes. It'll cost you your life (15:27).

Don't show partiality or favouritism (28:21). Particularly not to evil people, because it deprives the innocent of justice (18:5). Don't condemn the innocent or acquit the guilty (17:15, 24:24). You'll be cursed by entire peoples and condemned by entire countries (24:24).

Innocent people can be identified by the Godliness of their ordinary life (21:8), and vice versa. If you sow injustice, you'll reap ruin and disaster for yourself (22:8). Convict the guilty, and you'll be loved and receive blessings in return (23:25). If you gain a reputation for good judgment, you'll win favour and luxury (13:15). The rebuke of a wise judge to a person who will listen and take it to heart is previous and of great value. It's like a gold earring or a gold ornament. (25:12).

Criminals' accomplices become their worst enemies because they are witnesses who can testify against them about what they did. But when they are sworn in to court and forced under oath to recount, they are scared to speak (29:24).

False testimony is a serious matter of life and death which God hates (6:18). It is a terrible weapon which is lethal (25:18). Corrupt witnesses who lie laugh at the justice system and make a mockery of it (19:28). Deceitful witnesses end up dead (19:5, 19:9). Those who concentrate and listen carefully are trusted for their public testimony (21:28). Tell the truth as a witness, and do not lie to create a smokescreen (12:17, 14:5). It saves people's lives (14:25).

Do not crush vulnerable or needy people in court. God will become their lawyer and judge against you (22:22). When you do sue in court, don't gossip or betray secrets told to you in confidence. The person you betray may hear it may attack you, causing the judge to side with the other party (25:9-10). Be careful about impulsively suing someone for something you saw. It may well not have been what you thought. And that person may well have seen you doing something and mistakenly judged you too (25:8). If you take an idiot to court, all you are going to get is indignant rage, arrogant derision, and zero peace (29:9).

Leadership

As there are the wise, simple, and fools; there are good leaders, weak leaders, and bad leaders. Nations collapse because they have no guidance. Without good leadership and direction, countries fall to pieces (11:14).

The number of loyal followers a leader earns is what produces their glory. If you don't have any, you're no-one (14:28). They are always dealing with sycophants and people wanting special and favourable treatment (19:6). Everyone competes to plead their case and be listened to (29:26).

Leaders carry the weight of the world on their shoulders. When they smile, it means life and favour. It's so refreshing and relieving, it's like a rain cloud in spring (16:15). They should speak in a visionary way about the future, and never, ever further injustice (16:10). They should hate criminality and immorality, and their leadership should have a moral foundation (16:12). They should love honest people who speak with integrity and place enormous value on those who speak truthfully and morally (16:13).

A leader's direction and thoughts are ultimately controlled by God, which He targets to benefit those He loves (21:1). His security of position comes from his love and faithfulness, and cleaning out corrupt deputies. If the people he leads and governs know he loves them, challenges to his position are minimized (20:28). Removing evil people from official roles secures his position through that goodness. It's the same way a silversmith refines his raw material to make ornaments (25:5).

The heart of a good leader is so full of wisdom and alien to ordinary people it's comparable to the height of the stars and and the depth of the earth (25:3). A good one is always looking to drive out evil people, even from among the good (20:8-9, 20:26). When the evil are driven out, virtuous people prosper (28:28). His favour and goodness is like sweet refreshing dew on the grass (19:12). Skilled investigation of important matters brings them great praise (25:2).

The election of a good leader prompts elation and celebration (28:12, 29:2), and if they hate income or status derived from crime they will stay in their post for a long time (28:16). They provide stability by administering justice (29:4), which ultimately comes from God (29:26). If they treat poor people fairly, their position in the world will be immortalised in remembrance of it (29:14).

Leaders always want the best of everything; the best quality and workmanship, the best materials, and the most diligent suppliers. If you're skillful in what you do, they will seek you out and poach you to work exclusively for them (22:29). They choose the best people to be their friends. Someone they can see loves others who are good-hearted and speak gracefully (22:11).

It's completely inappropriate and shameful for authority and command to be inverted. Leaders who allow their subordinates to rule over them are disastrous (19:10). A good leader keeps order. Those who don't are taken advantage of and overthrown by rebellious disrupters. If that carries on, a symptom of it is a lot of leaders coming and going (28:2).

A servant, male or female, who gets to the top or usurps their superior is a disaster (30:22). Nobody wants or expects any of them to lie (17:7). Fining an innocent person is bad enough, but severely punishing honest officials is a truly stupid and immoral thing to do (17:26). If a leader listens to lies, it corrupts all his officials downstream and leads them into evil (29:12) such as seeking out bribes, which can destroy an entire country (29:4). Leaders should not drink, in case they forget what they've ruled or decided when under the influence. It could end in oppressed or poor people losing their rights (31:4-7).

A leader's wrath is so terrifying it's like the roar of a lion which can be heard for miles (19:12, 20:2) and angering them can cost you your life (20:2).

When an evil leader assumes power helpless people run and hide (28:12, 28:28). It's like being tyrannised by a roaring lion or a charging bear (28:15), and one of their markers is extortion (28:16). The people under them are utterly miserable (29:2), and moral sin explodes among the population (29:16).

Leaders who oppress the poor are like rain which destroys crops, instead of feeding them, they poison and destroy (28:3). Stay clear of angry and bad-tempered leaders. It could save your life, because their anger might lead them to sending you to your death. Wise people know how to calm them down (16:14).

VIII

10 Minute Guides

Even the smallest amount of time swimming in the wisdom of Proverbs is enough to produce enormous changes and benefits in a person's life.

Help For Right Now

Sometimes you need help right at this second and don't have time for hours of reflection. Life happens in real time trapping you on the defensive, requiring you to act immediately. Even if you are evil, wisdom can help you. If you are fool, it can give you the appearance of thoughtfulness. Often it is a case of *not* doing something, rather than doing something; if they want it now, the answer is no, but given time it is a *maybe*. Many of our mistakes are a result of impulsivity, rather than neglect. In these circumstances, discipline and self-control are the best course.

Get away from danger.

If you can see danger, run from it and find refuge (22:3, 27:12).

Discern who you are dealing with.

Evil people want to murder those who are good (29:10, 29:27). Fools won't learn (26:11). Adulteresses seek and lure their prey (7:9, 23:28).

Do not engage in evil.

Get away from evil people (1:19). Have nothing to do with any evil or criminal behaviour (13:20).

Shut up, listen, and appear thoughtful.

If you're not sure what to do or say, shut up (10:19, 11:12, 17:28). Listen instead (18:13). If you need to reply, ask for time to reflect or speak well of others recognised to possess good motives (22:11). *This will solve 99% of all problems you may face.*

Don't undertake any agreements, guarantees, or vows.

Don't shake hands on any deal or contract. Don't make any vows or enter into deals requiring a commitment you haven't scrutinised (11:15, 17:18). Be suspicious of flattery (29:5).

Respond gently.

Speak quietly in a amicable voice (15:1) and do not provoke conflict by exchanging anger (17:14).

Be self-disciplined and restrain yourself.

Don't take another glass or eat any more (21:17). Stop napping and get up to work (19:15, 20:13). Close your eyes and ears to sexual provocation (27:20).

Seek advice.

Ask for time to think. Ask as many provably wise, trusted advisers as possible to establish a consensus of opinion between them all (11:14, 15:22, 20:18, 24:6). Listen to them.

Emergency Surgery This Week

You need to turn your life around today. Maybe this week. But certainly, soon. As soon as you can. There are things you can stop doing, right now, today, which could make a miraculous difference in your life. Some are catastrophic, and others are chronic. You need to do them regardless of the negative consequences or price you feel you may pay.

Stop all evil behaviour or criminality.

Run away from evil and anyone involved in evil (3:7, 4:14). It's a matter of life and death (1:19, 3:31, 11:19. 24:1). Go *now*. Immediately. This *second*. Don't delay. It doesn't matter what you have to give up or the cost you have to pay. If you don't, you will lose everything. Do whatever you have to do, right now, to get away and never come into contact again. If you have evil friends, get away from them. If you are involved in doing evil, stop immediately. If evil you are oppressed by evil people or their deeds, leave.

Stop all unethical unbehaviour or immorality.

If you are abusing the poor, stop immediately (22:22) even if it costs you everything. Stop giving or receiving bribes (15:27, 17:8); stop withholding things as a miser (11:24, 11:26). Get away from radicals or revolutionaries (24:21-22). Stop scheming or approaching situations in bad faith (13:15). Get out of business dealings which are predicated on unjust ways of making money (16:8, 28:6).

Disconnect from any involvement in adultery or lust.

If you are married - even in name or on paper only - and are emotionally, sexually, or romantically involved with anyone other than your legal spouse, stop immediately and disconnect entirely. Permanently, with no exceptions or explanations (6:32-34). If someone is inviting you to commit adultery with them, run as fast as you can in the other direction (5:8, 7:25). If you are paying for prostitutes (29:3), chasing promiscuous women (6:25), or deceiving yourself you can control the spread of fire (6:27-28), stop immediately.

Stop drinking.

Alcohol will nullify the abilities you require for turning your life around, and increase the problems you already have (23:20-30). There is no reason for it other than cloaking your misery (31:6-7).

Own up and ask for mercy.

If you are in a hole, stop digging. Don't attempt to cover up what you've done (5:21, 15:3, 20:27). Take responsibility, renounce your own wrongdoing, and ask those you have injured for forgiveness (28:13).

Ditch the bad company.

You become like the people you spend time with. Hang around with the fools, and you will become a fool; spend time with the wise, and even if you don't become wise, you will benefit from their wisdom. Disconnect from all friends and associates who are evil, foolish, naive, lazy, or prone to scoffing. You'll be better off with no friends at all for now than a friend in one of them.

Get yourself out of any agreements, vows, or guarantees.

Don't sleep until you have removed yourself as a surety from anyone else's debt (6:3-5). Cancel the wedding, the event, or the undertaking you are unsure you are able to commit to (20:24).

10-Point Long-Term Operational Strategy

Being successful in life means choosing a path and adopting a strategy of how to live. It won't avoid trouble or tragedy, but wisdom will bring the benefits and longevity most people dream of which the Creator intended. A ten-thousand foot view of how to behave, what to do, where to go, and how to correct oneself is no simple task, given the depth and breadth of Proverbs. However, its themes can be summarised and compressed somewhat as marker posts on the map.

Your life will reflect your heart in the same way water reflects your face (27:19).

1. Get your relationship with God straight.

Believing this all appeared randomly is idiotic (Psalms 14:1, 53:1). Refer to God and trust Him. Agree with Him (3:5-6). His way is a refuge (10:29).

Fearing God means *humility*: fear, respect, and reverence. (1:7, 9:10, 14:16, 22:4, 24:21). It also means to hate evil, pride, arrogance, and vile speech (8:13). Just fearing Him means you are on the right track (14:2, 15:33, 16:6, 28:14) and behind the walls of a powerful fortress which will protect your family and children (14:26), turn you away from lethal traps (14:27, 19:23, 29:25), and be a fountain of life (14:27, 16:22, 19:23).

Put aside all your own notions and exclusively trust God to guide you down it (3:5-6, 16:21, 20:24, 23:19) to prosperity (28:25). Correction and instruction will be like a lamp providing light (6:23). You make the plans, and God carries you along the route He has planned for His own purpose (16:9, 19:21, 20:24).

2. Choose to walk uprightly and suppress your pride.

People have sets of ways they walk in, and life is a choice between these (2:9-10, 2:20, 20:24). Your way might seem right, but what you can't see is it leads to death (14:12, 16:25, 21:2, 21:16). You have a choice. To spend your life trying to live well and make good decisions (4:26-27, 16:1, 20:11), or to not bother and end up in disaster due to your own lack of sense (1:32-33).

Upright means living defined by God's thinking and standards, not our own (3:7, 19:16), and eternal life with Him (12:28). It means what is morally right, just, and fair (2:9). Seeking it will bring you favour (11:27), and those who do end up finding love and faithfulness (14:22); life, prosperity, and honour (21:21); living lives free of blame which straighten the road for their children (20:7).

You won't prosper if your motives are bad, and they come from the heart (17:20). The unfaithfulness of duplicity brings ruin (11:3) because it's a trap caused by evil desires (11:6). Pride, arrogance, and haughtiness are an engine and factory for sin (21:4). The root problem is always the same: *pride*

(13:10).

3. Choose your friends carefully.

If you spend time with fools, you will become a fool and end up being harmed for it (13:20). Everyone claims to be loyal and faithful, but it's genuinely hard to find people who genuinely are (20:6). Choose your friends carefully (12:26). Having the wrong friends means you pick up traits which bring ruin (10:17). Being corrupted by going along with evil people is catastrophic (1:8-19).

Flee from those who evil (3:7, 4:14), lazy (10:17), adulterous (7:6-9), or scornful (19:29). Be wary of those who are simple-minded (14:18). Avoid those who are gossips (11:13), foolish (13:20), fairweather (18:24), hot-tempered (22:24-25), alcoholic (23:21), tightfisted (23:6-8), lustful (31:3), revolutionary (24:21-22), won't tell you the truth (24:26), or insincere (27:6).

4. Choose your wife carefully.

A good wife is extremely rare and someone you should consider more valuable than the most precious jewel (31:10). It will be the most critical decision you ever make. She is such a blessing to a man she is like a royal crown on his head (12:4). The wrong wife is a catastrophic decision lasting a lifetime. A cold, mean-hearted wife is such a burden it feels like decay in your own bones (12:4).

Learn to recognise the character pf the *Adulteress*, and flee her like your life depends on it, because it does (2:18-19, 7:24-27, 9:14-17, 22:14).

Avoid anyone who sleeps in or drifts without purpose

(31:27), is chaotic or irresponsible (31:27), dresses poorly (31:22), is untrustworthy and fickle (31:11), is given to promiscuity or acute sexual behaviour (23:27-28), speaks harshly (31:26), doesn't know how to manage money (31:13-14, 32:24), or isn't charity or family-minded ((31:20, 12:4, 31:28-29).

5. Avoid debt, alcohol, conflict, laziness, and sexual immorality.

Death and destruction are never, ever satisfied. They always want more and more company (27:20). Careful what you put into your brain and body. If you feed on wisdom, you'll become wiser. If you feed on trash, you'll get sick and/or become a fool (15:14). When people don't have Godly counsel or revealed wisdom to instruct them, they stop trying to behave virtuously and indulge hedonistically in undisciplined sin (29:18).

Debt is slavery (22:7). Don't underwrite a debt security for any stranger outside your family (11:15, 17:18, 22:26). Don't shake hands on uncertain agreements (11:15, 17:18).

Don't drink heavily or indulgently (23:20). If you're numbing yourself from suffering, poverty, and misery, drinking has little purpose at all (31:6-7). It's best to stay away from alcohol if you can (20:1). Alcoholism ends in ruin and poverty (23:21).

Don't get involved in an argument which has nothing to do with you. You're asking for trouble, like grabbing a mad stray dog by the ears (26:17). Avoid arguments and trouble if you possibly can as it's the honourable way of dealing with them, Don't react instantly or rise to the bait (12:16, 19:11, 20:3). Deliberately picking a fight is like smashing open a dam. Drop the issue before the fighting starts (17:14).

Laziness is infectious (10:17) and it will make you sleep deeply (19:15, 20:13). It will make you poor (10:4, 20:13). Don't sleep too much. Even taking small day-naps folding your hands over your chest means poverty will strip you like an armed robber (24:33-34).

Lust starts with your attention being captured (7:10) through your eyes and what you are looking at (6:25). If you try to collect it in your lap, you'll get burned and be set alight (6:27). If you try to control it or conquer it, you'll lose and get burned (6:28). Stay away from a mistress, a prostitute, or a promiscuous woman (5:20). Adultery will get you killed (6:26) and prostitutes will destroy any wealth you build (29:3).

6. Speak carefully.

People hate and detest arrogant cynics, so be careful of how you appear to others (24:9). Speaking quickly or explosively is so foolish, there's more hope for the stupidest idiot (29:20).

To be wise, hold your tongue (10:19, 11:12) and only use it when your words will find favour and be received well (10:32). Restraint will save you from inadvertent disaster (21:23), and could save your life (13:3). Consider and weigh what you intend to say (15:28). If someone is angry with you, speak gently (15:1).

Don't use bad, nasty, or corrupt language like white lies and gossip. Keep it hygienically clean (4:24). Don't gossip (11:13), slander (10:18), tattle (11:13), or lie (10:18). Don't flatter people (29:5-6), make guarantees (20:22), or boast (27:1).

7. Earn a good reputation, faithfully.

Success is a result of understanding the importance of disciplining yourself (10:17) and valuing correction (15:5), as well as storing up wisdom and knowledge over time (10:14). People pour honour on those who are humble about their success and lowly in spirit (15:33, 18:12, 29:23), and those who loyally defend whom they serve (27:18).

The praise or admonition you receive will be in proportion to how prudent others recognise you to be (12:8). It's better to have a good reputation and be well thought of than to be rich. A good name is worth more than gold or silver, and it'll help you to re-earn both if you come to ruin (22:1). A good reputation and goodwill comes from being dedicated to being loving and faithful (3:4). If you gain a reputation for good judgment, you'll win favour and luxury (13:15).

8. Build wealth honestly, slowly.

Earned wealth comes from God (10:22) and are a result of wisdom (3:16), so give the first and best piece to God to honour Him (3:9). Wealth is built slowly, growing little by little, over a long time (13:11), and is a result of diligence (10:6, 28:20).

If you chase pipe dreams, you'll get nothing. If you put the physical labour in, you'll have plenty to eat (12:11, 28:19). If all you do is talk, you'll end up in poverty with nothing (14:23, 28:19). Hard work generates profit (14:23) and rewards (12:14). If you guard your labour and investment diligently, you will get to enjoy it in its fullness after it has grown (27:18).

Riches you get from fraud or criminality have no value (10:2), will drain away (13:11), and be stored for transfer to good people who live in a Godly way (13:22). You cannot become established through them (12:3). Don't take bribes. It'll cost you your life (15:27). It's better to be the lowest of the low with the poorest people than share in stolen goods with arrogant criminals (16:19). It's better to have a little as a Godly person than make a lot of money unjustly (16:8, 28:6).

9. Remember the poor and advocate impartial justice.

If you're cruel to the poor, or gloat over their suffering, you're insulting God, who made them and loves them. Be careful: God loves the poor, they are special to Him, and dismissing them will guarantee His wrath (14:31, 17:5). If you close your ears to their cries, you'll be ignored by God in return (21:13) and it'll be like receiving curse after curse (28:27). Be kind to them and you'll be blessed and marked out as a Godly person (14:21, 19:17) who lacks nothing (28:27). If you do, you're honouring God (14:31) and lending to Him (19:17).

Speak up for people who don't have a voice or are destitute (31:8-9). God hates the condemnation of the innocent (17:15), false testimony (6:18), and the acquittal of the guilty (17:15). Do not crush vulnerable or needy people in court. God will become their lawyer and judge against you (22:22).

Don't show partiality or favouritism (28:21). Speak up for the voiceless and defend their rights (31:8-9). A leader who gives them justice fairly will see his name immortalised in history (29:14).

10. Discipline your children as much as possible.

All children are born foolish and without any knowledge of the world (22:15). Harsh, loving discipline applied consistently erodes their inherent foolishness away over time and builds wisdom (22:15). Discipline is an act of love (3:12) and produces hope (19:18).

Wisdom is embedded into children by discipline and punishment. Warnings, rebukes, reprimands, and stern caretaking is what transforms them from foolishness to individuals of character (29:15). If you discipline them, they will delight you and give you peace (29:17). Severe discipline and punishment drives out evil from the inside (20:30).

If you love your children, you must discipline them as a matter of their life and death. If you spare them, you're not helping. It's actually hatred for them. A refusal to correct is a refusal to love and contributing to their death. (13:24, 19:18, 23:14). Don't hold back when you apply discipline and apply it as harshly as necessary because it won't kill them (23:13); on the contrary, it will save them from death (23:14).

Climbing Out Of Ruin

You're at rock bottom and don't know what to do. It all came crashing down, again. You're bankrupt, destitute, and at wits' end. The chances are your own foolishness and simple naivety were responsible.

The chances are it was no accident or random occurrence. If you're still stubborn after dozens of collapses and rebukes, there will come a day when your life simply falls apart, seemingly by surprise, and can't be repaired. There's an endpoint to the mistakes. (29:1).

Ruin is predictable.

Did you refuse to flee from danger (22:3, 27:12)? Were you stupid enough to invite it (17:19)?

Have you been evil, sought out evil, loved evil, or done evil (2:22, 10:30, 11:20, 12:7, 14:11, 17:11)? Did you take bribes (15:27), or offer them (17:8)?

Did you commit adultery (2:18-19, 5:5, 7:27, 9:18), waste your money on prostitutes (29:3), or become intoxicated with lust (6:27-28)? Did you sleep too much (6:9-11), ignore being diligent in your work (10:6), or collapse into laziness (10:4, 20:13)?

Did you chatter foolishly (10:10), rashly (21:23), lie (11:5, 11:9), give false testimony (19:5, 19:9), or open your mouth without guarding it (13:3)?

Did you act in bad faith (13:15), with duplicity (11:3), secure a stranger's debt (22:26-27), or become deceived by flattery (26:28)?

Did you ignore instruction (13:18), lack guidance (11:14), talk instead of doing (14:23), impulsively run into something without thinking it through (21:5), or refuse to get advice and counsel (15:22)?

Were you cruel (11:17), miserly or stingy (28:22), put your trust in riches instead of God (11:28), or withhold what you were able to give (11:24, 11:26)? Did you oppress the poor (22:16), ignore the cries of the poor (28:27), or sow injustice (22:8)?

Did you live recklessly (19:16), lack self-control (25:28), waste your money on gifts for the rich (22:16), fall in love with pleasures like alcohol and fine foods (21:17), or fall into drunkenness and alcoholism (23:21)?

Did you anger a leader (20:2, 16:14), exalt yourself in powerful company (25:6-7), or join the cause of troublemakers and revolutionaries (24:21-22)?

Did you have fairweather friends (18:24), foolish children (19:13), or victimise your own parents (20:20, 30:17)?

Is the root problem your pride (15:33, 18:12, 29:23)?

Start with God.

All wisdom starts with understanding who God is and how powerful He is. Understanding his position as the Creator and author of all life, compared to yours as a simple primate who cannot change their own nature by themselves. The right response is humility: fear, respect, and reverence. (1:7, 9:10, 14:16, 22:4, 24:21). It means to hate evil, pride, arrogance, and vile speech (8:13). Just fearing Him means you are on the right track (14:2, 15:33, 16:6, 28:14) and behind the walls of a powerful fortress which will protect your family and children (14:26), turn you away from lethal traps (14:27, 19:23, 29:25), and be a fountain of life (14:27, 16:22, 19:23).

Don't try to figure things out on your own. Refer to God and trust Him. Agree with Him (3:5-6). His way is a refuge (10:29). Before all else, tell Him even the smallest of your plans and ask Him to bless them, so He can agree and establish the successful end result (16:3).

You should do all you can possibly do in your own capacity to succeed. Prepare everything as diligently as you are able to in the greatest detail. But ultimately, the end result, the decision of victory or loss is up to God. Control over the whole situation and victory itself belongs to Him (21:31).

Don't try to deceive God or deny what you know. He guards your life and can see everything. He'll pay you back exactly for what you've done (24:12). Hardening your heart, or turning against Him, will send you down the wrong road land you in trouble (28:14).

Don't blame God. Take responsibility.

Innocent people can be identified by the Godliness of their ordinary life (21:8), and vice versa. People deceive themselves about their own goodness and their good faith (16:2). It's not God's fault you screwed up. You have no case against Him and no right to be angry with Him (19:3, 19:27).

The consequences of not making any effort to become wise are severe: disaster striking, calamity overtaking, and being overwhelmed with distress and trouble (1:26). It's so severe it's similar to a storm or a whirlwind. (1:27).

Life is about cause and effect, and you always end up taking the consequences for your own behaviour in the same way a farmer reaps the harvest he sows (1:31, 11:31, 20:11, 22:8). Your decisions and choices bear fruit over time which you will be forced to eat (1:31).

If you pay back evil for good, or bad faith for good faith, evil will never leave you or your home. You've ensnared yourself without knowing (17:13). Cruelty will bring you ruin (11:17), as will gloating after you've won (24:17).

Your own duplicity, caused by the snare of your own evil desires, are what caused your troubles (11:3, 11:6, 12:8).

It's your fault. You are responsible.

Banish your pride.

Humble people receive honour for their character and things they achieve. As pride precedes and provokes ruin, the opposite is also true: humility precedes and provokes honour. People pour honour on those who are humble about their success and lowly in spirit (15:33, 18:12, 29:23), and those who loyally defend whom they serve (27:18). Never praise yourself (27:2).

Big leaps or boasts of pride or haughtiness are always followed by disgrace (11:2, 16:18, 29:23).

It's better to have nothing and fear God, than to be filthy rich and unable to sleep at night (15:16), speak in a vile way (19:1, 19:22), or be evil (37:16).

Are you Simple (10:13)?

Confess and own up.

If you are in a hole, stop digging. Don't attempt to cover up what you've done (5:21, 15:3, 20:27). Take responsibility, renounce your own wrongdoing, and ask those you have injured for forgiveness (28:13).

Love and faithfulness make amends for injuries (16:7), so speak in a soft, gentle voice (15:1).

Get as much advice and counsel as you can.

Get advice. Lots of it. (20:18). You can secure victory by getting truthful counsel from a lot of different advisors. The more opinions you get, the more likely you are to recover (11:14, 15:22, 20:18, 24:6). If you don't get counsel or advice, you'll stay where you are, in ruins (15:22). Wise people listen to advice (12:15, 13:10).

If you spend time with wise people, you will become wise for it (13:20). Listen to the people who tried to stop you idiotically stumbling towards your own death and ruin (24:11).

Stop the stupid things.

It will keep getting worse. Death and destruction are never, ever satisfied. They always want more and more company (27:20). Run away from evil and anyone involved in evil (3:7, 4:14). It's a matter of life and death (1:19, 3:31, 11:19. 24:1). Run from adultery (5:8, 7:25).

Shut up (10:19, 11:12, 17:28). Listen instead (18:13). Do

not provoke conflict by exchanging anger (17:14). Don't take another glass or eat any more (21:17). Stop napping and get up to work (19:15, 20:13). Close your eyes and ears to sexual provocation (27:20).

Get rid of bad friends (12:26) because behaviour is infectious (13:20). Having the wrong friends means you continue being influenced by the traits which brought you to ruin (10:17).

Accept correction.

What's the point of praying to God for help when you won't follow the simple instructions of your parents and friends? Your prayers are detestable (28:9).

God can and will fix mistakes, so forget your ideas and trust completely in Him (3:5-6). He will stop you from being snared in traps (3:26). He disciplines his children out of love like any parent who cares about their future (3:12). If you are on the receiving end, listen humbly and don't lash out or be resentful. Be grateful for it, it's the proof you are His and He delights in you (3:11).

If you heed instruction, you'll profit from it and be rewarded. If you ignore instruction and advice, you'll suffer for it (13:13, 13:18). You may even die (21:16). The difference between wisdom and foolishness is the ability to accept instruction and correction. Listen to advice and respect those who are wiser than you. If you do, you will end up being one of them (19:20). If you take in correction, you'll grow smarter, and be at home with wise people; counted as one of them (15:31).

A rebuke you give to a wise person is welcomed (9:8-9) and goes in deeper than a hundred lashes goes into a fool (17:10). The rebuke of a wise judge to a person who will listen and take it to heart is previous and of great value. It's like a gold earring or a gold ornament. (25:12).

You can learn to be wise. (1:23, 22:17-19, 23:12) It means to think about the right way to live (14:8) and the right steps to take (14:15). The first steps to start with are consistently fearing God (1:7, 14:16, 22:4, 23:17); listening to your parents' teaching (1:8), and avoiding any involvement with evil people (1:10-19, 14:16).

Choose to walk uprightly.

Choose wisdom, not scheming (10:23). The right road ahead is straight and well-established, but all the wrong ways are crooked and go nowhere (2:13, 4:11). If you make that wise choice, you should look straight ahead and not go left or right (4:25-26), and put aside all your own notions and exclusively trust God to guide you down it (3:5-6, 16:21, 20:24, 23:19) to prosperity (28:25). Correction and instruction will be like a lamp providing light (6:23).

Discipline is what will save you, or keep you from falling into traps and death (5:22, 22:5). If you hate it, you hate yourself (15:31).

Stay focused and keep your eyes on the wise course of action (17:24). Hard work generates profit (14:23) and rewards (12:14).

IX

Handling Common Situations

How do you apply the broad wisdom of Proverbs to the common types of situations most people will face before mid-adulthood?

Making New Friends

Guard your heart (4:23) and choose your friends carefully (12:26). Everyone claims to be loyal and faithful, but it's genuinely hard to find people who genuinely are (20:6). Having the wrong friends means you pick up traits which bring ruin (10:17). Being corrupted by going along with evil people is catastrophic (1:8-19).

The purpose of friendship is sharing burdens (17:17), and the authenticity of one can be measured by the gentle heartfelt honesty of advice shared in return (9:8-9, 24:26, 27:9).

It's easier to filter out who you should *not* be friends with. Do not develop friendships with those who are:

- Gossips (11:13)
- Foolish (13:20)
- Fairweather (18:24)
- Hot-tempered (22:24-25)
- Tightfisted (23:6-8)
- Revolutionary (24:21-22)
- Averse to telling you the truth (24:26)
- Insincere (27:6)

The signs of a good potential friend include that they:

- Never refuse to help (3:27)
- Will rebuke you (9:8-9)
- Are able to keep secrets (11:13)
- Resemble a brother (17:17)
- Overlook faults and flaws (17:9)
- Rescue you from your own stupidity (24:11)
- Have strong boundaries (25:17)
- Are faithful as a person (25:19)
- Offer blunt honesty, gently (24:26, 27:6)
- Make you smarter (27:17)

What character do your new friend(s) have? Do they appear to be a Fool, or Wicked?

If you spend time with wise people, you will become wise. If you spend time with fools, you will become a fool and end up being harmed for it (13:20).

Being Seduced By Lust Or Flattery

Lust starts with your attention being captured (7:10) through your eyes and what you are looking at (6:25). Women are everywhere. Be careful where you look. Your eyes always want more and more and more because they can never stop (27:20).

We are seduced by smooth talk (2:16, 5:3, 6:24, 7:5, 7:21, 22:14). Be careful who you are talking to and what you are listening to. When someone is flattering you, they're setting you up for a fall which will bring you to ruin if you buy into it (26:28).

Lust is like fire. It grows like fire and spreads like fire. If you try to collect it in your lap, you'll get burned and be set alight (6:27). If you try to control it or conquer it, you'll lose and get burned (6:28).

Your sexuality is for your wife, and her alone (5:15-19).

Defusing A Quarrel Or Rivalry

The root cause of any conflict is always pride (13:10). Bad feeling and confrontation is provoked by hatred (10:12), anger (29:22), impulsive temper (15:18), greed (28:25), gossip (16:28), over-familiarity (25:17), or jealousy (27:4).

Certain characters love conflict and try to produce it wherever they can: the unfaithful (13:2); twisted, evil people (6:14, 16:28); divisive gossips (30:33); the hot-tempered (14:17); and revolutionaries (24:21-22).

If a person is hot-tempered, leave them to it. Let them learn the hard way (19:19). Wise people reject conflict and turn it away (29:8).

Don't get involved in an argument which has nothing to do with you. You're asking for trouble, like grabbing a mad stray dog by the ears (26:17). If you try to intervene to stop stupid people behaving foolishly, expect to be mauled (17:12) and met with hostility (9:7-8).

Probing too deeply into painful things can end up in you covered in dirt or dishonour (25:27). Avoid arguments and trouble if you possibly can as it's the honourable way of dealing with them, Don't react instantly or rise to the bait (12:16, 19:11, 20:3). Don't rise to being unnecessarily or unfairly insulted when you never deserved it. You have nothing to fear. It's as fleeting as a tiny bird which doesn't land (26:2).

Wise people finalise and end conflicts by calming things down and bringing peace (29:11). It's calmed by patient middlemen and mediators who don't react and wait for the anger to relent (15:18, 19:11)

Arguments and fights need fuel to continue or restart, as fires need wood or charcoal. Their fuel is gossip and the aggressive behaviour of high-conflict people. Take away the fuel and the fire will go out. (26:20-21). High-conflict troublemakers like cynics, complainers, and sarcastic bullies are often the source of arguments and insults which incubate fighting. Get rid of them and peace will return (22:10).

To calm someone down who is angry, speak in a soft, gentle voice (15:1), and to soothe someone who is extremely angry, give them a gift in secret; a financial bundle will definitely change their mood (21:14).

If multiple parties can't agree, roll a dice and use randomness for allocation and priorities to soothe the friction (18:18).

Doing Someone A Favour

Give without thinking about holding back portions for yourself (21:26, 22:9).

Never forsake or abandon a friend, or a friend of your family (27:10); never withhold help if you can give it (3:27). Rescue people idiotically stumbling towards their own death and ruin (24:11). If you refresh others, they will reciprocate and refresh you when you need it (11:25). But don't expect loyalty or faithfulness in return, regardless of how someone promises it (20:6).

Don't take vows lightly or impulsively. You'll get trapped in them not having thought things through (20:25).

Don't underwrite a debt security for any stranger outside your family (11:15, 17:18, 22:26), because it's a trap you've fallen into created by your own mouth (6:1-2). If they can't pay, you could lose your own home, or the bed underneath you which you sleep on (22:26-27).

If you get a reputation as a generous person, you'll always have plenty of people trying to take advantage of you (19:6).

Starting A Relationship

All relationships start with friendship. Does this person gently offer blunt honesty, (24:26, 27:6), make you smarter (27:17), rebuke you (9:8-9), have strong boundaries (25:17), and overlook your mistakes gracefully (17:9)?

Or are they a gossip (11:13), hot-tempered (22:24-25), tightfisted (23:6-8), foolish (13:20), fairweather (18:24)?

Have realistic expectations. A wife is extremely difficult to find (31:10) and loyalty is rare (20:6). Be careful your lust has not been set alight by what you've seen with your eyes (6:27), or the smooth talk you've heard (26:28).

Beauty is fleeting. It doesn't matter how beautiful a woman is if she's crass or stupid. It's like a gold ring on a pig (11:22).

A woman who could make a good wife:

- Is purposeful and reliable (31:27)
- Dresses in a classy way (31:22)
- Speaks gently, sparingly (31:26)
- Handles money well (31:13-14, 32:24)
- Is chaste (23:27-28)
- Is family-minded (31:28-29)

Never, ever engage in adultery (6:26), and beware of the

Adulterous Woman. She dresses sexually (7:10) and lures you in boldly (7:13) with her words (2:16, 7:5, 7:21). She wanders (5:6) and lays in wait (23:28). Learn to recognise her disguise or you'll die (2:18-19, 5:5, 7:27, 9:18).

Don't spend yourself emotionally and financially on women. They can ruin leaders and powerful people (31:3). Your own wisdom is like having a sister or relative with you at all times giving you great advice (7:4).

Starting A New Job

If in doubt, shut up (10:19, 11:12, 30:32) and listen (18:13). Keep your cards close to your chest (12:23). You'll appear thoughtful (17:28).

Your boss's attitude towards you will be based on your character and behaviour. If you act wisely, they will love you and delight in you. If you're foolish and act shamefully, their anger will get worse and worse over time, emerging eventually as fury (14:35). Protect him, and you'll receive honour (27:18). Don't slander another loyal worker or fellow employee to him. He'll condemn you and punish you for it (30:10).

Don't honour yourself, and wait to be called on (25:6-7). Then speak gracefully and gently (25:15), making clear your love of good people with pure motives (22:11).

If you are slack in your work, you let down your friends and colleagues. It's destructive to others and like a form of vandalism (18:7). Sleeping when it is time to work is disgraceful (10:5). Lazy people are so obnoxious to employers they are like the taste of raw vinegar, or smoke in the eyes (10:26).

The praise or admonition you receive will be in proportion to how prudent others recognise you to be (12:8). A good reputation and receiving good will comes from being dedicated to being loving and faithful (3:4) . If you gain a reputation for good judgment, you'll win favour and luxury (13:15).

Attending A Lavish Event

When you have dinner with a powerful person, the food is a trap. Don't stare in awe, and don't eat much. If you're hungry or a glutton, put a knife to your throat to stop yourself if you have to. Your appetite and manners are being watched (23:1-3).

The praise or admonition you receive will be in proportion to how prudent others recognise you to be (12:8).

Don't exalt yourself or honour yourself. Don't claim a place in the inner circle. Both of those things will end up in you being humiliated in front of everyone. Wait to be invited or called for (25:6-7). If you want to persuade, you need to employ patience. It will only happen that way. Speak gently. It's more powerful than you think. (25:15).

Control your lust like your life depends on it (6:25) and avoid alcohol (20:1). Don't boast about tomorrow. You have no idea what it may bring (27:1).

Certain types of speech are not wanted or expected from different people (17:7). Be careful of what you say and be mindful of the words others hear from out of your mouth. Don't use bad, nasty, or corrupt language like white lies and gossip. Keep it hygienically clean (4:24). Speak gracefully, and make clear your love of good people with pure motives (22:11).

Good conversation feels wonderful. The right words at the right time are pure joy (15:23), and an honest answer is like a kiss on the lips (24:26).

It's better to be an ordinary small businessman with a small number of employees than to act important when you don't have money to eat. Don't fake it to make it (12:9, 13:7). Don't spend money giving wealthy people gifts which they don't want or need, because you'll end up ruined and poor (22:16).

Everyone wants to be friends with the rich because of the freebies it means they can benefit from (11:6). Appearances can be deceiving: rich people often dress down to avoid attention so you never know who you could be talking to (13:7).

Ending A Relationship

Everything in your life flows from your heart. Guard it. (4:23).

Get away from evil people (1:19). Have nothing to do with any evil or criminal behaviour (13:20). Stay away from adultery at all costs and don't go near that person's house (5:8, 7:25).

The wrong wife is a catastrophic decision lasting a lifetime. A cold, mean-hearted wife is such a burden it feels like decay in your own bones (12:4). A wife who constantly argues and quarrels is exhausting and feels like the water-drip torture of a roof endlessly leaking on your head (19:13, 27:15). You'll be better off living somewhere as inhospitable as the desert (21:19), or on the far corner of the roof of your house than share the building with her (21:9, 25:24). Restraining her is impossible; it's like trying to grasp liquid in your hand or holding back the wind (27:16).

Duplicity brings ruin (11:3). Humility will bring you wisdom (11:2), and kindheartedness will bring honour (11:16) which benefits you (11:17). Don't lead people on (3:28). If you've screwed up, 'fess up. If you're in a hole, stop digging. Don't try covering up, or digging yourself out (28:13).

People are clumsy and often hurt you (18:24). If someone is injured or offended, they can become as unyielding as the stone walls of a military city in a terrible war (18:19).

Nasty, vile speech can crush a person's morale and spirit (15:4). If you use words recklessly they pierce a person like a sword (12:18) and ignite quarrels (15:1). Speak quietly in a amicable voice (15:1) and do not provoke conflict by exchanging anger (17:14).

When Your Heart Gets Broken

Everything in your life flows from your heart. Guard it. (4:23). Everyone has their own pain and joy only they feel and experience. Yours won't be the same as others, and vice versa (14:10). Some days, celebrations may ironically end in tragedy (14:13).

Don't be jealous of those who get their way by hurting others (3:31). People are clumsy and often hurt you (18:24).

If you're heartbroken, your spirit will feel crushed (15:13). It can feel like it's deep in your bones and they've dried up (17:23). It feels unbearable (18:14). Anxiety and worry weighs your heart down (12:25).

A miserable, mean heart means a miserable life 15:15). If you burn with resentment and envy, it'll feel like your bones are rotting inside you (14:30). Don't swear revenge or payback (24:29). Pride, arrogance, and haughtiness are an engine and factory for sin (21:4).

The purpose of friendship is to share troubles with one another so the burden of them is lessened (17:17). Seeing a happy face with a cheerful heart brightens anyone up like a powerful medicine (15:13, 17:22). Lovely smells and lotions bring joy to the heart (27:9).

Your own stupidity can lead to your ruin. Take responsibility. It's not God's fault you screwed up. You have no case against Him and no right to be angry with Him (19:3, 19:27). If you've screwed up, 'fess up. If you're in a hole, stop digging. Don't try covering up, or digging yourself out (28:13).

Careful with alcohol. Beer and wine help relieve people's suffering, poverty, and misery (31:6-7) but it will take more than it gives (23:32).

Signing A Contract

Don't take vows lightly or impulsively (20:24). Keep secrets faithfully and be trustworthy (11:13). Contracts are required because human beings aren't loyal or faithful, and must be constrained by law (20:6).

Make sure you are not dealing with evil people (1:19). Have nothing to do with any evil or criminal behaviour (13:20). Don't enter agreements with revolutionaries (24:21-22).

Duplicity brings ruin (11:3). as does approaching situations in bad faith (13:15). If you sow injustice, you'll reap ruin and disaster for yourself (22:8).

Be aware of flatterers. They're acting in bad faith and softening you up (29:5). People cover up their ulterior bad motives with kisses (27:6).

Don't underwrite a debt security for any stranger outside your family (11:15, 17:18, 22:26), and if someone you don't know puts up collateral for a stranger, get a deposit. They're going to lose it (20:16, 27:13).

To determine someone's character, look at a person's ordinary life more broadly. It will be displayed in their background and everyday dealings (21:8).

Business must always be honest and be of the utmost integrity. Scales and measures must be just, fair, and accurate under all circumstances because God is Holy (11:1, 16:11, 20:10). Don't use dishonest scales or measurements (11:1, 16:11, 20:10, 20:23). Initial complaints may be exaggerated so they can negotiate the price down. Once they've got their discount, they'll run home to boast about it (20:14).

If you don't get counsel or advice, you'll fail (15:22). Wise people listen to advice (12:15, 13:10). Keep your own counsel and your cards close to your chest. Don't boast or over-share. (12:23). Choose middlemen who relay messages for you carefully. An evil will bring trouble, and but one you can trust heals the situation (13:17). Using a fool is so perilous it's like cutting off your own feet or drinking poison (26:6).

Unexpected Fame Or Success

The nature of someone's character is tested by who they become once they are given fame and praise. In the same way you refine silver in a crucible and gold in a furnace, the pressure of adoration and applause tests who you are (27:21).

Humble people receive honour for their character and things they achieve. As pride precedes and provokes ruin, the opposite is also true: humility precedes and provokes honour. People pour honour on those who are humble about their success and lowly in spirit (15:33, 18:12, 29:23).

If you put your trust in wealth instead of God, or you're eager to run after money, you will fall and come to ruin (11:28, 28:20). Don't be naive or under any kind of illusion: wealth and riches bring more trouble with them than their benefits (15:16). Big leaps or boasts of pride or haughtiness are always followed by disgrace (11:2, 16:18, 29:23).

Stay focused and keep your eyes on the wise course of action (17:24), which is fearing God (10:22), wisdom (3:13-15), and your reputation (22:1). It's far better to be wise than to be rich (3:13-15). Give the first and best piece to God to honour Him (3:9). Be kind to the poor and you'll be blessed and marked out as a Godly person (14:21, 19:17) who lacks nothing (28:27).

Choose your friends carefully (12:26) because behaviour is

infectious (13:20). Dress down to avoid attention (13:7). You can be sure you'll have a lot of friends (14:20, 19:4); everyone wants to be friends with the rich because of the freebies it means they can benefit from them (11:6). You are vulnerable to being held hostage through lawsuits and extortion which are like a ransom on your life (13:8).

Rich people deceive and delude themselves in a circular way: because they have wealth, they are convinced it is evidence of their own wisdom and virtue. Once you have some wealth, you'll wrongly come to think of it as a fortress or a fortified city nobody can overcome, where you're safe (10:15, 18:11).

If you oppress the poor to increase your wealth, you'll come to ruin and poverty (22:16) because God is their defender of their fields (23:10-11). Your success can cause you to speak harshly and unsympathetically to poor people who often beg you for mercy (18:23).

Discipline is what will save you, or keep you from falling into traps and death (5:22, 22:5). If you hate it, you hate yourself (15:31). Never praise yourself. Let an outsider do it for you (27:2). Be suspicious of anyone flattering you. They're setting you up (29:5). Store luxury goods up instead of consuming them impulsively (21:20). Beware of sexually predatory women (7:9, 23:28). Don't squander money on women in general (31:3), and never prostitutes (29:3). Careful what you put into your brain and body. If you feed on wisdom, you'll become wiser. If you feed on trash, you'll get sick and/or become a fool (15:14).

Don't make grandiose proclamations, like swearing revenge on someone publicly (20:22), or boasting confidently about what tomorrow will bring (27:1).

Do things in logical, practical ordered steps which make

sense. Priorities and dependencies. First deal with the work which provides the harvest of your income and means. Then build what you want. Only start on your house after you have planted your fields first (24:27).

Receiving Correction

The key difference between a fool and a wise person is their willingness to accept correction (1:7). A fool is defined by their refusal to acknowledge or receive any form of correction *at all*.

Listen to it. Do not ignore it (8:33). It is a lamp for your footsteps (6:23).

To love correction is to love wisdom itself, and to hate it is foolish (12:1). To ignore it means you hate yourself. If you listen, you'll get smarter (15:32). Your prosperity will increase directly in line with how willing you are to accept instruction (16:20).

Where there is consensus on something, there is collective wisdom (11:14).

Wise people welcome correction even if it hurts. They know it makes them smarter, and they listen. They love the person who corrects them and love being corrected. It increases their affection for the person reproving them. Sarcastic and evil people hate it and attack (9:7-9).

Discipline produces hope (19:18). God disciplines his children out of love like any parent who cares about their future (3:12). If you are on the receiving end, listen humbly and don't lash out or be resentful. Be grateful for it, it's the proof you are His and He delights in you (3:11).

If you never receive correction, you are doomed (13:24, 19:18, 23:14). You'll end up bringing shame to your family from your foolishness (29:15). Discipline should never be held back and be applied as harshly as necessary because it won't kill you(23:13); on the contrary, it will save you from death (23:14).

Starting A Business

Before all else, tell God even the smallest of your plans and ask Him to bless them, so He can agree and establish the successful end result (16:3).

There's no secret here: if you chase pipe dreams, you'll get nothing. If you put the physical labour in, you'll have plenty to eat (12:11, 28:19). If all you do is talk, you'll end up in poverty with nothing (14:23, 28:19). Smart people act, and don't just keep their wisdom in their head (13:16). Wanting something intensely but lacking the wisdom to get it won't get you anywhere. You'll simply miss the target faster than if you didn't care (19:2).

Get advice. Lots of it. (20:18). The more opinions you get, the more likely you are to succeed (11:14, 15:22, 20:18, 24:6). If you don't get counsel or advice, you'll fail (15:22). Wise people listen to advice (12:15, 13:10).

Hard work generates profit (14:23) and rewards (12:14). Bad work gets paid with a bad check; good work gets solid pay (11:18). Smart planning done patiently, and diligently, generates profit, whereas running into things quickly bankrupts you (21:5). If you guard your labour and investment diligently, you will get to enjoy it in its fullness after it has grown (27:18).

Do things in logical, practical ordered steps which make

sense. Priorities and dependencies. First deal with the work which provides the harvest of your income and means. Then build what you want. Only start on your house after you have planted your fields first (24:27).

Make sure you have high quality equipment for producing what you plan to. If not, you won't have a harvest (14:4). Always know the exact condition of your investments, accounts, and resources, at all times. Give them extremely careful attention in great detail. Then you will have all the things your family and employees need (27:23-27).

Don't use dishonest scales or measurements (11:1, 16:11, 20:10, 20:23). Don't hire lazy people (10:26) or fools (26:10). Don't delay returning things unnecessarily, delay repayment (3:28), or withhold what you can give (11:24, 11:26).

Wealth and success are built slowly, growing little by little, over a long time (13:11). A good reputation and goodwill from others comes from being dedicated to being loving and faithful in business (3:4). It's better to be an ordinary small businessman with a small number of employees than to act important when you don't have money to eat. Don't fake it to make it (12:9, 13:7).

Starting With Savings & Wealth

Don't exhaust yourself trying to get rich or rely on your own cleverness (23:4). If you put your trust in wealth instead of God, or you're eager to run after money, you will fall and come to ruin (11:28, 28:20).

Focus on these things above money, as they give you the means to earn it: fearing God (10:22), wisdom (3:13-15), and your reputation (22:1). Invest in truth, wisdom, instruction, and insight and do not sell even a piece of them (23:23).

There are three ways to become wealthy: a) inherit cash and property directly through one's parents (19:14), b) generating it dishonourably through fraud, exploitation, or criminality (10:2, 11:16), and c) earning it honestly, little by little, over a long time (13:11). Only the third kind lasts and it comes from God (10:22). It is a long-term by-product and fruit of wisdom itself (8:18).

If you chase pipe dreams, you'll get nothing. If you put the physical labour in, you'll have plenty to eat (12:11, 28:19). If all you do is talk, you'll end up in poverty with nothing (14:23, 28:19). Smart people act, and don't just keep their wisdom in their head (13:16).

Smart planning done patiently, and diligently, generates profit, whereas running into things quickly bankrupts you

(21:5). Whenever you make money or produce a harvest, give the first and best piece to God to honour Him (3:9). Your prosperity will increase directly in line with your generosity (11:25, 22:9) and how willing you are to accept instruction (16:20). The more you give, the more you will get back (11:24).

The difference between poverty and wealth is the faithful diligence you put into your work consistently over time. Diligence brings wealth (10:6, 28:20) and luxurious living (12:27) which fully satisfies (13:4). If you guard your labour and investment diligently, you will get to enjoy it in its fullness after it has grown (27:18). Always know the exact condition of your investments, accounts, and resources, at all times. Give them extremely careful attention in great detail (27:23-27).

Hiring Someone

Choose your employees and workers carefully (12:26). Don't put your hope in men (11:7, 29:25) or trust in yourself, it's foolish (28:26). People aren't generally faithful or loyal, but they always claim to be. It's incredibly hard to find someone who is (20:6).

A boss's attitude towards their worker is based on their character and behaviour. If they act wisely, you will love them and delight in them . If they're foolish and act shamefully, your anger will get worse and worse over time, emerging eventually as fury (14:35).

Whoever you hire will affect others. One person sharpens another in all ways, as you use iron to sharpen an iron sword (27:17). If you hire wise people they will make more wise people, and vice versa (13:20).

You should love honest people who speak with integrity and place enormous value on those who speak truthfully and morally (16:13). Their character will be displayed in their background and everyday dealings (21:8). Don't show partiality or favouritism (28:21).

Select wise people who listen to advice (12:15, 13:10). A rebuke you give to a wise person is welcomed (9:8-9) and goes in deeper than a hundred lashes goes into an idiot (17:10).

Be suspicious of anyone flattering you. They're setting you up (29:5). Don't have anything to do with revolutionaries (24:21-22). Loners and unfriendly people are selfish. They spurn the necessity of relationships with others and often deliberately pick fights (18:1). Don't hire high-conflict, hot-tempered people (22:24-25).

If you hire divisive stirrers and gossipers, you will get conflict, quarreling, and strife which will only be fixed by expelling them mercilessly (22:10). The worst is an employee, male or female, who gets to the top or usurps their superior (30:22).

Laziness is so destructive to others it is like a form of vandalism (18:7). Sleeping when it is time to work is disgraceful (10:5). Don't hire lazy people. They are so obnoxious to employers they are like the taste of raw vinegar, or smoke in the eyes (10:26). If you hire a fool, they will injure everyone around them like an archer shooting and wounding at random (26:10). It is so perilous it's like cutting off your own feet or drinking poison (26:6).

Choose middlemen and workers who represent you carefully. An evil messenger will bring trouble, and but one you can trust heals the situation (13:17). Light in their eyes will bring happiness and joy to the recipient (15:30). Their trustworthiness and integrity refreshes the sender's spirit like a cold drink of snow water in the heat of harvest (25:13).

Being Tempted With A Shortcut

Success is a result of understanding the importance of disciplining yourself (10:17) and valuing correction (15:5), as well as storing up wisdom and knowledge over time (10:14). Smart planning done patiently, and diligently, generates profit, whereas running into things quickly bankrupts you (21:5). Choose wisdom, not scheming (10:23). The more you give, the more you will get back (11:24).

Rules and commands are there for a reason. Follow them, and you'll be OK. Ignore them to live recklessly, and it will end up with you dying (19:16). Don't take vows lightly or impulsively. You'll get trapped in them not having thought things through (20:25). Don't lead people on (3:28)

Duplicity brings ruin (11:3). as does approaching situations in bad faith (13:15). If you sow injustice, you'll reap ruin and disaster for yourself (22:8). If you pay back evil for good, or bad faith for good faith, evil will never leave you or your home. You've ensnared yourself without knowing (17:13).

Don't take bribes. It'll cost you your life (15:27).

Don't offer bribes. Offering a bribe to someone feels good. Like a magic spell or a faultless plan which can never fail (17:8).

Don't use dishonest scales or measurements (11:1, 16:11, 20:10, 20:23).

Lying and false testimony will get you into a lot of trouble. You'll be found out, be punished, and imprisoned. You might even lose your life (11:5, 11:9). Don't use your speech to mislead others with false testimony about someone who hasn't wronged you (24:28).

If you oppress the poor to increase your wealth, you'll come to ruin and poverty (22:16) because God is their defender (23:10-11).

Lust is dangerous. It is evocatively described as playing with fire or hot coals; there is no safe way to handle it without severe consequences (6:27-28). It starts with what you're looking at (5:19, 6:25, 7:10). Your eyes are never satisfied, always wanting more and more (27:20).

Stay away from adultery at all costs because it's a matter of life and death (2:18-19, 5:5, 7:27, 9:18).

When A Relative Dies

Some days, celebrations may ironically end in tragedy (14:13). All people die, and death is both guaranteed and constant (27:20). God sees it all, even bodies in graves and the fires of Hell (15:11). Everyone has their own pain and joy only they feel and experience. Yours won't be the same as others, and vice versa (14:10).

Grief is painful. If you're heartbroken, your spirit will feel crushed (15:13). It can feel like it's deep in your bones and they've dried up (17:23). It feels unbearable (18:14). Anxiety and worry weighs your heart down (12:25).

Long life is from God (8:35), and a result of remembering teaching and keeping commands (3:1-2), guarding one's heart (4:23), fearing the Lord (10:27), righteous Godly living (11:18), a peaceful heart (14:30). Our soul is like a lamp God placed inside us which illuminates who we truly are at our deepest depth (20:27).

But above all, a long, well-lived life comes from wisdom (3:16), and it is crowned by grey hair (16:31).

Parents leave their houses and fortune to their children to pass on generational wealth (19:14). A wise employee will be given part of childrens' inheritance as one of the family, particularly if there's a bad child they end up in charge of and favoured ahead of (17:2). If an inheritance is claimed too soon, even just early, it won't end up in increased prosperity over the long term (20:21).

Be strong for others when someone dies. If you fail, flounder, or collapse when it counts, your weakness is an embarrassment (24:10).

After Making A Tragic Mistake

Are you a Fool? Are you Simple? Are you Lazy, Sarcastic, or Wicked?

Your own stupidity can lead to your ruin. Take responsibility. It's not God's fault you screwed up. You have no case against Him and no right to be angry with Him (19:3, 19:27).

Stay away from anyone foolish who helped you into ruin (14:7). Disconnect from anyone you are involved with who is evil (1:19) or adulterous (5:8, 7:25).

If you're still stubborn after dozens of collapses and rebukes, there will come a day when your life simply falls apart, seemingly by surprise, and can't be repaired. There's an endpoint to the mistakes (29:1). What's the point of praying to God for help when you won't follow the simple instructions of your parents and friends? Your prayers are detestable (28:9).

People deceive themselves about their own goodness and their good faith (16:2). You won't prosper if your motives are bad, and they come from the heart (17:20). Wherever you find it, the root problem is always the same: *pride* (13:10).

If you're impulsive, explosive, or otherwise lack self-control, you're as vulnerable as a strong fortress citadel whose walls have been broken through. Your defenses are down and you will be routed by people looking to overcome you (25:28). Big leaps or boasts of pride or haughtiness are always followed by disgrace (11:2, 16:18, 29:23). God will tear down the source of your pride (15:25).

Good speech helps virtuous people escape trouble (12:6). Confess and renounce your sins and errors and you'll find forgiveness and mercy. Don't attempt cover-ups (28:13).

An offended close friend won't give in or lower their guard. They are so entrenched they are like a city in a war protecting itself (18:19), but love and faithfulness make amends for injuries (16:7).

Put down your pride (13:10).

Listen first. Don't cut someone off or provide the answer before hearing the situation or question (18:13). To calm someone down who is angry, speak in a soft, gentle voice (15:1), then give an gift honestly (18:16). To soothe someone who is extremely angry, give them a gift in *secret*; a financial bundle will definitely change their mood (21:14).

If the person is hungry, feed them. If they are thirsty, give them a drink. Your goodness will take them completely by surprise and earn God's favour towards you. It's like throwing burning coals over their head, all for you to get the reward for discontinuing the conflict (25:21-22).

God can and will fix mistakes, so forget your ideas and trust completely in Him (3:5-6). He will stop you from being snared in traps (3:26).

Becoming A Father

Children come from God, and are a *gift* from God. They are a *reward* from Him to you from the womb (Psalm 127:3). They are a crown for your parents, their grandparents (17:6). All children are born foolish and without any knowledge of the world (22:15).

A father's purpose is to use his authority responsibly to instruct and command his children (22:15). His wisdom is like royal garments and jewelry his child wears throughout their life (1:7-8). He wants the best for his children (23:26) and leaves his houses and fortune to his children to pass on generational wealth (19:14).

Your job is to start them off on the right path (22:6) by disciplining as God does, because of how he cares about his children's futures (3:12). Harsh discipline is a matter of their life and death, and produces hope (19:18). If you discipline them, they will delight you and give you peace (29:17). Severe discipline and punishment drives out evil from the inside (20:30). It won't kill them (23:13); on the contrary, it will save them from death (23:14).

God is a protection and refuge for your child, as He is for you (14:26).

Taking A Calculated Risk

Ricks aren't automatically foolish. The difference between wisdom and foolishness is the ability to accept instruction and correction (19:20). It is *recklessness* which ends up with your death (19:16) and big leaps or boasts of *pride* which are followed by disgrace (11:2, 16:18, 29:23).

Risks need strength and vigour which are the natural advantage of young men and bring them glory (20:29). Complex things are only done through wisdom. They only exist because of wisdom (24:23). Wisdom is more important than strength, and intelligence is far more powerful than anything else (24:5). Delight in it rather than human scheming (10:23). Discipline is what will save you, or keep you from falling into traps and death (5:22, 22:5).

Before all else, tell God even the smallest of your plans and ask Him to bless them, so He can agree and establish the successful end result (16:3). You make the plans, and God carries you along the route He has planned for His own purpose (16:9, 19:21, 20:24). Prepare everything as diligently as you are able to in the greatest detail. But ultimately, the end result, the decision of victory or loss is up to God. Control over the whole situation and victory itself belongs to Him (21:31).

Smart planning done patiently, and diligently, generates profit, whereas running into things quickly bankrupts you (21:5). Keep your own counsel and your cards close to your chest. Don't boast or over-share. (12:23). Don't make grandiose proclamations or brag confidently about what tomorrow will bring (27:1)

Get advice. Lots of it. (20:18). You can secure victory by getting truthful counsel from a lot of different advisors. The more opinions you get, the more likely you are to succeed (11:14, 15:22, 20:18, 24:6). If you don't get counsel or advice, you'll fail (15:22). Wise people listen to advice (12:15, 13:10).

Do things in logical, practical ordered steps which make sense. Priorities and dependencies. First deal with the work which provides your income and means. Then try to do what you want. Only start on the big thing after you have prepared the ground underneath it first (24:27).

Make sure you have high quality equipment (14:4). Always know the exact condition of your investments, accounts, and resources, at all times. Give them extremely careful attention in great detail (27:23-27). Don't use dishonest scales or measurements (11:1, 16:11, 20:10, 20:23). Don't offer bribes (17:8) or take bribes. It'll cost you your life (15:27).

Wisdom will only be good beforehand as prevention, and be no help or cure after the inevitable happens (1:26).You'll take the consequences if it goes wrong, so be prepared to (1:31, 11:31, 20:11, 22:8). If you screw up, confess. Ask for forgiveness. Don't attempt cover-ups (28:13).

If you succeed, be humble about your success and lowly in spirit (15:33, 18:12, 29:23). Never praise yourself. Let an outsider do it for you (27:2).

Dealing With Abusive Family

If you can see immediate danger, run from it and find refuge (22:3, 27:12). Get away from evil people (1:19).

The happiness of your home can make or break your life and it will show up publicly (21:8). It's better to have a small serving of food made with love than a huge feast created alongside hatred and resentment (15:17). It's better to have unappetizing dry bread in peace and quiet than hours of feasting in a house where everyone is quarreling (17:1). Everything in your life flows from your heart. Guard it. (4:23).

Nasty, vile speech can crush a person's morale and spirit (15:4). If you use words recklessly they pierce a person like a sword (12:18) and ignite quarrels (15:1). Hope for something which keeps being put off as a relentless disappointment makes you sick and depressed (13:12).

Abusers who look for fights invite their own ruin (17:19). The insults and arguments from cynics and critics stir up entire cities with bad feeling and conflict (29:8). Wherever you find it, the root problem is always the same: *pride* (13:10).

Don't react instantly or rise to the bait (12:16, 19:11, 20:3). Don't rise to being unnecessarily or unfairly insulted when you never deserved it. You have nothing to fear. It's as fleeting as a tiny bird which doesn't land (26:2).

If you burn with resentment and envy, it'll feel like your bones are rotting inside you (14:30). Don't swear revenge or payback (24:29). Pride, arrogance, and haughtiness are an engine and factory for sin (21:4).

Parents are required to use harsh discipline upon their children, for their benefit; imitating God and His love for His children. Real discipline is a product of love (3:12), and is *not* mindless authoritarianism.

God examines our internal motives (16:2, 20:27, 21:2, 24:12), and the subsequent choices we make (5:21, 20:27). Be careful about what you label "abuse": don't use your speech to mislead others with false testimony about someone who hasn't wronged you (24:28). If conflict and confrontation is unavoidable, get advice and guidance. Get lots of it (20:18, 24:6).

Fighting In Court

Justice comes from God (29:26). A correct ruling in court is wonderful. It's like apples made of gold, embedded in silver (25:11).

Be careful about impulsively suing someone for something you saw. It may well not have been what you thought. And that person may well have seen you doing something and mistakenly judged you too (25:8). If you take an idiot to court, all you are going to get is indignant rage, arrogant derision, and zero peace (29:9).

Riches make you vulnerable to being held hostage through lawsuits and extortion which are like a ransom on your life (13:8).

Get advice. Lots of it. (20:18). You can secure victory by getting truthful counsel from a lot of different advisors. The more opinions you get, the more likely you are to succeed (11:14, 15:22, 20:18, 24:6). If you don't get counsel or advice, you'll fail (15:22). Wise people listen to advice (12:15, 13:10). Choose middlemen who relay messages for you carefully. An evil one will bring trouble, and but one you can trust heals the situation (13:17).

Be patient. If you fly off the handle and lose your temper easily, you'll look stupid (14:29). If in doubt, shut up (10:19,

11:12, 30:32) and listen (18:13). Keep your cards close to your chest (12:23). You'll appear thoughtful (17:28). Those who concentrate and listen carefully are trusted for their public testimony (21:28).

Don't gossip or betray secrets told to you in confidence. The person you betray may hear it and attack you, causing the judge to side with the other party (25:9-10).

Tell the truth as a witness, and do not lie to create a smokescreen (12:17, 14:5). False testimony is a serious matter of life and death which God hates (6:18). It is a terrible weapon which is lethal (25:18). Corrupt witnesses who lie laugh at the justice system and make a mockery of it (19:28). Deceitful witnesses end up dead (19:5, 19:9).

Do not crush vulnerable or needy people in court. God will become their lawyer and judge against you (22:22).

Facing Up To Alcoholism

Alcohol relieves people's suffering, poverty, and misery (31:6-7). Addiction, habituation, and sin don't discriminate. They condemn anyone and everyone; even entire countries (14:34). Only fools consume trash (15:14).

People who linger over alcohol, staring at the sparkling liquid in the glass, and getting a taste for it, end up with suffering, sadness, arguments, complaints, needless bruises, and bloodshot eyes (23:29-30). Alcohol causes people to collapse into poverty and ruin because of the constant drowsiness it causes (23:21). It feels like constantly being bitten and poisoned by a viper (23:32).

Know the symptoms when you one is too many and ten is not enough: hallucinations, confusing thoughts, unexplained injuries, stupor (23:33-35); waking up in the morning searching for a drink (23:35). Death and destruction are never, ever satisfied. They always want more and more company (27:20).

Your own stupidity can lead to your ruin. Take responsibility. It's not God's fault you screwed up. You have no case against Him and no right to be angry with Him (19:3, 19:27). Your lack of self-discipline is make what made you as vulnerable as a strong fortress citadel whose walls have been broken through. Your defenses are down and you have been routed. (25:28)

If you're still stubborn after dozens of collapses and rebukes, there will come a day when your life simply falls apart, seemingly by surprise, and can't be repaired. There's an endpoint to the mistakes. (29:1).

God can and will fix mistakes, so forget your ideas and trust completely in Him (3:5-6). He will stop you from being snared in traps (3:26).

Confess and renounce your sins and errors and you'll find forgiveness and mercy. Don't attempt cover-ups (28:13). Stay away from anyone foolish who helped you into ruin (14:7).

> *First you take a drink,*
> *then the drink takes a drink,*
> *then the drink takes you.*
> *(F. Scott Fitzgerald, 1896 - 1940)*

Processing Your Anger

Fools are volatile and hot-headed, yet completely confident in their stupidity (14:17). They don't hold back or restrain the full extent of their arrogant rage and lash out immediately (29:11, 14:3), flaring up in irritated anger the second they feel annoyed (12:16). They loudly blurt out all their thoughts and feelings instead of being discrete (12:23), and erupt into arguing and quarreling almost instantly (20:3).

Anger ends in cruelty (27:4) because fury overwhelms a person (27:4). It feels like a torrent (27:3-4), and evil people expect it (11:23). It is infectious (22:24-25), so do not be friends with angry people. It will affect your body and be visible (14:30). so to counter it, wise people reject it and turn it away (29:8). Wherever you find it, the root problem of anger always the same: your *pride* (13:10).

Being hot-tempered will cause you to do and say stupid things (14:17). If you like fighting and quarreling, the real problem is you love sin. If you go out there advertising you are ready for a fight, you're inviting ruin (17:19). Deliberately picking a fight is like smashing open a dam. Drop the issue before the fight starts (17:14). Speaking quickly or explosively is so foolish, there's more hope for the stupidest idiot than someone who allows themselves to (29:20). Restraint will save you from inadvertent disaster (21:23), and could save your life (13:3) as leaders who get angry are deadly (20:2). Being slow to fury helps calm the situation down (15:18).

Everything in your life flows from your heart. Guard it. (4:23). Your life will reflect your heart in the same way water reflects your face (27:19). Hardening your heart, or turning against God, will send you down the wrong road land you in trouble (28:14). People hate and detest arrogant cynics, so be careful of how you appear to others (24:9).

If you burn with resentment and envy, it'll feel like your bones are rotting inside you (14:30). Don't swear revenge or payback (24:29). Don't publicise that you'll take revenge. Let God avenge you. (20:22), but don't gloat or rejoice when your enemies lose (24:17). Cruelty will bring you ruin (11:17).

Be careful when drinking alcohol if you're angry, because things never end up well (20:1).

Don't react instantly or rise to the bait (12:16, 19:11, 20:3). Don't rise to being unnecessarily or unfairly insulted when you never deserved it (26:2). Don't use your speech to mislead others with false testimony about someone who hasn't wronged you (24:28). Take a breath when people address you harshly (15:1), and make sure to stay away from gossip (16:28) and jealousy (27:4).

If your enemy is hungry, feed him. If he's thirsty, give him a drink. Your goodness will take him completely by surprise and earn God's favour towards you. It's like throwing burning coals over his head, all for you to get the reward for discontinuing the conflict (25:21-22). If you're patient and overlook an offence, your glory will be on display (19:11).

If conflict and confrontation is unavoidable, and you have to go to war as a last resort, get advice and guidance. Get lots of it (20:18, 24:6).

Being Falsely Accused Or Betrayed

False testimony is a serious matter of life and death which God hates (6:18). Calumny is a terrible weapon which is lethal (25:18). He hates the condemnation of the innocent (17:15) and the false testimony of whisperers (6:18) specifically. Those who engage in it are cursed by entire peoples and condemned by entire countries (24:24). Sly cynical chatter will earn you horrified looks from people. It's like a wind from the north bringing unexpected stormy rain (25:23).

Duplicity brings ruin (11:3). as does approaching situations in bad faith (13:15). Don't deride people who live nearby and trust you (11:12), plot against them (3:29), or make baseless accusations about people who have not harmed you (3:30, 24:28). Those who dream up evil schemes are hated for it (14:17). Don't gossip (11:13), slander (10:18), tattle (11:13), or lie (10:18). That includes misusing language to avoid offense with long words and long obscure vocabulary (10:17).

Bosses will condemn and punish a person for defaming a loyal worker or good employee to them (30:10). Deceitful witnesses end up dead (19:5, 19:9).

Be patient. If you fly off the handle and lose your temper easily, you'll look stupid (14:29). Don't react instantly or rise to the bait (12:16, 19:11, 20:3). Don't rise to being unnecessarily or unfairly insulted when you never deserved it (26:2).

If you burn with resentment and envy, it'll feel like your bones are rotting inside you (14:30). Don't swear revenge or payback (24:29).

If you're patient and overlook an offence, your glory will be on display (19:11). The first person to speak always seems right. Until what they say is scrutinised by their opponent (18:17).

Justice comes from God (29:26). He hates seven things specifically: pride, lying, bloodthirstiness, scheming, enthusiasm for evil, false witnesses spewing defamation, and divisiveness (6:16-19). Slanderers always end up being punished, given enough time (19:5).

If conflict and confrontation is unavoidable, get advice and guidance. Get lots of it (20:18, 24:6).

Undertaking Leadership

Leadership is difficult (16:15) and is controlled by God (21:1).

Leaders should hate criminality and immorality, and their leadership should have a moral foundation (16:12). They should love honest people who speak with integrity and place enormous value on those who speak truthfully and morally (16:13). They should never, ever further injustice (16:10).

The number of loyal followers a leader earns is what produces their glory. If you don't have any, you're no-one (14:28).

A good leader:

- Is celebrated when they are assume office (28:12, 29:2);
- Prioritises order and continuity (28:2);
- Treats poor and vulnerable people fairly (29:14);
- Provides stability by administering justice impartially (29:4);
- Hates criminality and immorality (16:12);
- Is even tempered (16:14) but terrifying when wrathful (19:12, 20:2);
- Loves honest people who speak with integrity (16:13);
- Speaks in a visionary way about the future (16:10);
- Drives out evil people, even from among the good (20:8-9,

20:26) so virtuous people prosper (28:28);

- Carries out skilled investigation of important matters (25:2).

In the same way a silversmith refines his raw material to make ornaments, he removes evil people from official roles to secure his position (25:5).

Leaders should not drink, in case they forget what they've ruled or decided when under the influence. It could end in oppressed or poor people losing their rights (31:4-7).

X

Filling The Gaps

Not all of us grew up with parents who taught us what we needed to know to survive or prosper. You don't always know what you should know or didn't learn.

What You Should Have Been Taught

Where you are in life

You weren't born special or clever. You were born foolish (22:15). Where are you now at this moment as a person (12:15)? What kind of person are you? Did you continue to become a Fool (13:16)? Did you become Lazy (26:14), Sarcastic (21:24), or Wicked (1:16)? Or are you just Simple (21:11)? Do you need God's discipline (5:23, 28:4)?

Who you belong to

Everything that exists belongs to God, including you (22:2). Your mind, body, and soul belong to God (15:9). You belong to your parents. You belong to your siblings. You belong to your wider family. Your friends choose you to belong to them. You belong to a school. You belong to a church. When you marry, you belong to your wife, your children, and your grandchildren. All of which belong to God. *Do you feel like you belong to anyone, when you are God's possession?*

How cause and effect works

The purpose of discipline is to make someone aware of the severity of their behaviour and its consequences (11:17). Punishment is exacting a price as repayment for an offence (1:31). When the person is aware, or the price has been paid, the process is over. The product being your own ability to discipline yourself as an adult (11:17). If your parents did not discipline you, over-disciplined you, or confused punishment for discipline, it is you who reaps what they sowed (22:8, 29:15). *Do you know and appreciate what you are responsible for, and how what the effects in your life have you as their cause?*

When to say no

Manipulative adults train children to be frightened to say no, by intimidating them with the threat of harm or ominous loss of approval. *As an adult, do you know how to say no to evil people (1:10)?*

How to learn

God is the source of all learning (1:7). Free public libraries are next. Where do you find out what to do (14:8), and how do you know what you don't know (15:31-32)? *Do you know how to study or where to get the materials? Do you know how to learn and accept correction?*

How and when to disconnect from your family

God is a family (Gen 1:26). The purposes of family are multiplication (Gen 1:28), support (Gen 2:18), discipleship (Deut 6:6-7, 22:6), belonging (John 8:35, Ps 68:6), provision (1 Tim 5:8), and protection (14:26). The aim of effective parenthood is the healthy separation of a child as a functioning independent new adult human (22:6). Western societies prescribe the age of eighteen as the average threshold when a person should have reached the maturity necessity to cater to their own survival. *Do you know the right way to disconnect from them and become your own person, particularly if your family is broken?*

How to avoid serious danger

Do you know when someone or something could kill you (22:3)? Do you know how to recognise it and flee from it? *Or do you think it is funny, edgy, or pleasurable?*

What your natural gifts are

What talents do you naturally have (3:9-10)? What skills and practices do you have a natural aptitude for? Have you discovered them all, or are there some lying dormant you could uncover? *What could they do for your life (18:16)?*

What your profession is

A trade or a profession is a necessary set of skills for a specific purpose, in which you are qualified through examination. With them, you pursue a vocation or occupation, in which you make a living by being employed to undertake daily labour in a series of roles or individual jobs (28:19). Over time, these form the track record of a career which determines your prosperity (22:29). *What would be your role on a desert island with only twenty survivors? What is your profession?*

Which tools you need for daily life

Do you have a resume? Do you books to consult when you don't know (15:14)? Can you write up a monthly budget for groceries (21:5)? Do you know how to detect "red flags" in people you won't ignore (14:6)? Can you file a tax return? Do you know how to tick off a to-do list? Do you have a productivity system for getting things done (21:5)?

Who to seek advice from

If you don't get lots of advice, you will fail (15:22). Do you know the difference between good advice and bad advice (12:15)? Do you know the types of people who will offer either of these? Advice is often painful correction. *Are you willing to accept correction (10:17, 15:32)?*

How to find role models

God is always your role model to follow (9:10). Human role models are your flawed Earthly heroes (29:25). The example you wish you were like (13:20). They are people to copy who got it right. *Can you list three people you admire? Are the people you admire fools, or evil?*

How to find mentors

God is always your mentor (9:10). A human mentor is someone you know who is already qualified, and has experience in, something you want to do (13:20). Not a coach, but someone you can consult on why you got it wrong when you tried (27:6). *How can you find someone you look up to and trust, who can advise and correct you?*

How to speak

Your tongue has the power of life and death (13:3, 18:21). Words must be used in a timely way which is appropriate (25:11), to different types of people (23:9). Do you speak like a fool, a scoffer, or someone who is evil? *What do you use your words for?*

The qualities you want your wife to have

It is extremely difficult for anyone to find a good wife, even if you are the wealthiest king in the world (31:10). A noble wife has a certain set of characteristics (31:10-31) which are opposite to a bad one (9:13–18). *Can you list the traits you are*

215

looking for in the most important investment of your life?

How to tell a good friend from a bad friend

It's much easier to find friends, and not all of them are good (4:14–19, 20:9). You will become like them (13:20). The wrong crowd will corrupt you and the selfish ones will use you for their own purposes (18:24). The right people will be your refuge and soldier brothers (17:17). *Do you know how to choose friends carefully, and discretely reject those who could bring you harm?*

How to spot people with bad intentions

People are rarely loyal (20:6). All of them are born fools. And many of them are evil, lazy, sarcastic, or simple (22:15). Can you spot behaviours in others which suggest they may want to harm you, or do not care about the damage they do to you as they pursue what they want (10:10)? *Do you know how to avoid them?*

How to stick up for yourself

There is no virtue in weakness (24:10). The world is full of people who could exploit you, deceive you, abuse you, or even kill you (13:20). If you allow them to take advantage of you, you will put others you are responsible for, at risk. Are you a doormat? Are you intimidated by criticism, disapproval, or terrified of conflict? *Have you practised how to respond to bullies?*

How and when to end a relationship

Only your relationship with God is eternal. Friendships and marriages start, and they end (21:9). They often go bad, and not always due to anyone's fault. Often parents are harmful people (22:24). Knowing how and when to end a relationship, despite the awareness of the painful grief to follow, is as important as knowing how to start and conduct one (4:14-19). *Do you know how to detach from someone without harming others, even if it will hurt?*

How to process a broken heart

Your heart must be protected because it is fragile and your life flows from it (4:23). When you experience any kind of loss, grief is the process by which it heals itself. Heartache is spiritually excruciating (14:30, 15:13). There is a healthy way of enduring grief (17:22), and a destructive one. *Do you know how you should protect yourself when you are vulnerable and hurt?*

How to create and manage a home

Furnishing and managing a house or apartment is labour-intensive and takes time. Doing it well is an act of love and takes a long time to learn (24:3-4). *Can you find your own accommodation and know what to put in it?*

How to present yourself

Humans respond to aesthetic signals. We recognise others by how they dress (Ecc 9:8), how proudly they stand (23:7), how their eyes move (16:30), the speed at which they speak, and the tastefulness of the choices they make (12:15). *What do you look like? How do others perceive you when you introduce yourself?*

How to keep yourself clean and healthy

Foul smell indicates disease. Scruffiness demonstrates indifference and disorder. Obesity suggests gluttony and greed. Your life displays your heart, and good stewardship of yourself lifts your spirit (3:7-8, 17:22). Your body, heart, and spirit all belong to God (Deut 10:14-17). *Is your body healthy?*

How to display manners

Manners are the means by which beasts (apes) signal their discipline, refinement, consideration, and good character. They help us show the moral virtue of our it, like honour and humility, to others (25:6). *Do you say please and thank you? Do you cut in line? Do you open the door? Do you keep people waiting?*

How to engage in a dinner event

We offer our hospitality to others to build and nurture friendship; as a gesture of warmth, community, and sacrifice (15:17). Children are fed; adults feed others. Can you lay a table and choose wine for the main dish? Do you know how to RSVP and dress (23:1-3)? *What gift will you bring (18:16)? What conversations can you bring pleasure to others in (25:11)?*

How to dance

Many babies can dance before they can speak. Dancing is a gift from God which is as natural an activity as breathing or speaking (Ps 149:3, Ecc 3:4). We formalise our dancing into technical maneuvers to enjoy together. *Can you do a few steps of Tango or Foxtrot?*

How to send correspondence elegantly

Words and speech differentiate us from beasts. A letter has a specific format, as does a postcard, an essay, a love poem (15:4), a tax return, a test message, or an email. *Do you know to devise an eloquent handwritten letter by candlelight for someone to savour, and enclose it formally in an envelope?*

How to dress and act on formal occasions

The clothes we wear are often uniforms, even if we sometimes call them *outfits*. They indicate our class, physique, and membership (25:6-7). We decide to wear specific uniforms together to mark different occasions, and temporarily adopt a style of performance to act out social pageantry. *Do you know the difference between Black Tie and White Tie? Do you know the names of the parts of the clothes?*

How to plan and set objectives

God sets your path, and you decide the steps (16:9). All of them should be committed to Him first for blessing (16:3) after taking as much advice/correction as possible (24:6). Do you know what you want? *On the map, where is origin A and destination B? How long will it take you to get there and how will you know?*

How to budget your time and money

Accounting is what you did in the past. Budgeting is what you plan to do in the future, according to what you think you will have (27:23). It is a way of limiting your time or your money to make the most prudent organisation of it (13:16). *Do you know how to stay within your limits to avoid ruin?*

How to manage debt

Debt is borrowing from the future and is difficult tool to manage. It can turn into a trap (22:7) and must be clearly bound to time limits. Borrowing should only done when it's not necessary. *Are you responsible enough to pay back on time?*

How to set personal limits and boundaries

Only God is able to be in all times and places simultaneously, and he enforces distinctions and boundaries (15:25). If you allow others to dominate your time, heart, or decisions, you will end up exhausted, ruined, and poor (25:28). Knowing when to stop, and when to say no, keep your heart healthy and spirit buoyant (4:23). *Do you know how to say no even under intimidation or emotional blackmail?*

How to work through a difficult decision

If you don't take advice on something you have no experience in, you will always fail (11:14). Friends help us reason through our difficulties and tell us the truth (27:9). There may not be a right answer, but wisdom is your lamp and God guides your path (20:24). *Do you know how to apply wisdom to a problem you don't know how to handle?*

How to control your temper

There are few situations, if any, where displays of anger make anything better. They make you look like a fool (14:29), destroy friendships (15:18), and put everyone in danger (29:22). *How do you control yourself when you feel unable to? Are you able to walk away when you feel like you don't want to?*

How to prioritise different things

Not everything or everyone is important. Some are more important, time-critical, or labour-intensive than others (24:27). *Do you know how to categorise and evaluate the importance of things? Do you have a way of ensuring they get done in the right order?*

How to confront betrayal

People are not loyal by default, and true friends are hard to find (20:6-8). Betrayal can be minimised by picking your friends carefully (12:26) and ensuring you do not entrust things too quickly with the wrong people (19:22-23). There is a right way to react (17:9), and a wrong way. *How should you respond when someone lets you down?*

How to cast your vote

Achieving a consensus among those who disagree is difficult, but extremely important to preserve order and happiness (11:14). There is no perfect system, only trade-offs and compromises to settle disagreements. *Do you know how to tell your leaders what you want?*

How to own up to mistakes and fix them

Mistakes and correction go hand-in-hand as an evolutionary learning system. Your ability to respond productively to correction defines you (28:13), not your predisposition to get it wrong. If you don't own up, you won't be successful (28:13). *Do you ask others for help and adjust your approach when trying again?*

How to control your lust

There is no "safe" way to "manage" sexual desire, as there is no way to hold burning coals (6:27-29). It intensifies when you fuel it, and only stops spreading by cooling it down. It can lead you to your death while presenting as pleasure (7:22). The only way is to contain it in the fireplace of marriage and express it towards your wife (5:18). *Do you know how to stop the fuel supply or put out the fire?*

How to avoid the negative effects of alcohol

Alcohol has no real purpose outside numbing misery (31:6-7). It just *is*. Intoxicants dull your wisdom and become dangerous when you use them as medication (20:1). *How bad are the consequences to you if you don't discipline yourself? Do you know when to stop?*

How to conduct yourself during employment

Workplaces have social customs. The excellence or indifference you show in the performance of your duties can be the difference between ruin or wealth (10:4–5). Do you know the rules of how to behave in a workplace with others, or how to discover them (10:26)? *Do you have a strategy or system for protecting your reputation and pursuing excellence which will cause others to seek you out?*

How to tell an adulterous woman from a Godly wife

Not all women are created equal; nor do they make the same choices or pursue the same aims (14:1). Their worst and best forms are clearly definable (11:16), and most girls are on a continuum of traits even for seasons of time (9:13). The wrong choice can lead to you to ruin and death (5:1-7), and the right one will be your greatest (12:4). *Are you able to recognise what marks out Lady Folly from the Noble Woman?*

How to build wealth

Money and success are not mysterious. They take time, diligence, and hard work (10:4, 13:11, 14:23, 21:17, 22:4, 27:23-27, 28:20). It happens in invisibly small steps, not overnight. You can make it fast dishonestly but it won't last (13:11). Wealth is a byproduct of wisdom and prudence, not luck (8:18-21). *Do you understand how wealth is built? Do you have a strategy to build it over the next forty years?*

How to deal with difficult people

Obnoxious people are an intractable law of nature, and are not going away any time soon. They can be categorised, and wisdom is about knowing how to navigate the damage they cause. In most cases, avoidance works (10:8). But when they cause conflict, you should develop skills for handling them (15:1). *Have you rehearsed responses to situation where you will be provoked by incompetence, stupidity, or defamatory insults?*

How to learn leadership

Great men are *bred*, even if they possess the character of a leader as a child (19:20). Good leaders have specific traits and aims, which they demonstrate in their actions towards those they steward and the fruits produced from them (14:28). God can teach you to be one (21:1), but you must first be His humble servant (22:4). *Do you know what a good leader is, why their authority can be trusted, or how to become a servant so you can lead others who may serve you?*

When You Don't Know Anything

Where you start in life, and the mistakes you make, aren't the end. Biography isn't destiny. We are all born foolish (22:15), and if we're lucky enough, we have parents who are wise enough to teach us wisdom (14:18). A significant proportion don't. They never grow out of their simplicity without enormous effort (1:22), which is fought through the emotional jungle of processing resentment over not being taught what they needed to know (15:12).

In biblical terms, to be unwise is synonymous with "lacking knowledge". To be wise is to accrue knowledge of the world and gain insight into it. It is not a moral judgment to lack knowledge, it is a factual *state* of being. You don't have the knowledge you need. You fix it by getting it (1:23, 22:17-19, 23:12), not via some automatic process during your sleep. The more you gain, the more sophisticated your insight becomes.

Sometimes you don't know anything at all and your life is a total mess. It can feel like you're adrift in a world you have no idea how to navigate at all. You were never taught navigation skills in the first place and don't know where to begin.

Lady Wisdom's words are aimed at *you*. Her call is for not to those who are already stable and successful. Read her words again.

*Let all who are simple come to my house! Come, eat my
food and drink the wine I have mixed. Leave your simple
ways and you will live; walk in the way of insight.*

Pursuing wisdom is a *choice*. You must choose such a path,
which is an act of wisdom in and of itself. If one were to study
the lives of people admired across the world, one would find a
common theme amongst them: *suffering*. Many of the greatest
role models began their lives with suffering; transitioned to
failure; but became someone extraordinary through the rod
of wisdom life disciplined them with over time. They lacked a
good beginning, like you.

- Ludwig van Beethoven grew up with an alcoholic father
  and lost his hearing.[10]
- Vincent van Gogh lived in poverty with mental illness.[11]
- Benjamin Franklin left school at a young age due to
  poverty.[12]
- Henry Ford grew up with an abusive father and dropped
  out of school.[13]
- Albert Einstein struggled in school and was thought to be
  mentally slow.[14]
- Thomas Edison was labeled "difficult" in school and was

[10] Solomon, M. (1998). *Beethoven*. Schirmer Books.

[11] Wallace, R. (2012). *The world of Van Gogh: 1853-1890*. Time-Life Books.

[12] Isaacson, W. (2004). *Benjamin Franklin: An American life*. Simon &
Schuster.

[13] Watts, S. (2005). *The people's tycoon: Henry Ford and the American century*.
Vintage.

[14] Calaprice, A., & Lipscombe, T. (2019). *Albert Einstein: A biography*.
Prometheus Books.

fired from jobs for lack of productivity.[15]

- Walt Disney was fired for "lack of creativity".[16]
- Levi Strauss lost both parents at a young age and survived an abusive upbringing.[17]
- Colonel Sanders failed at multiple businesses and was broke at sixty-five.[18]
- Richard Branson struggled with dyslexia and dropped out of school at sixteen.[19]
- Jim Carrey lived in a van with his family as a teenager.[20]
- Larry Ellison grew up in an abusive home and dropped out of college.[21]
- Sylvester Stallone struggled with poverty and homelessness.[22]
- Ralph Lauren grew up in a poor, dysfunctional family.[23]
- Ted Turner suffered emotional abuse from his father and

---

[15] Stross, R. (2008). *The wizard of Menlo Park: How Thomas Alva Edison invented the modern world.* Crown.

[16] Gabler, N. (2006). *Walt Disney: The triumph of the American imagination.* Vintage.

[17] Blaszczyk, R. L. (2019). *Levi Strauss: The man who gave blue jeans to the world.* University of Massachusetts Press.

[18] Lowe, B. (1970). *Life as I have known it has been finger lickin' good.* Creation House.

[19] Branson, R. (2011). *Screw business as usual.* Portfolio.

[20] Palliser, C. (2012). *Jim Carrey: The biography.* John Blake.

[21] Symonds, M. (2003). *Softwar: An intimate portrait of Larry Ellison and Oracle.* Simon & Schuster.

[22] Hofler, R. (2007). *The man who invented Rocky: The making of Sylvester Stallone's classic film.* Taylor Trade Publishing.

[23] McDowell, C. (2003). *Ralph Lauren: The man behind the brand.* HarperCollins.

dropped out of college.[24]

- Michael Jordan was cut from his high school basketball team.[25]
- Alan Gerry was raised in poverty and dropped out of high school.[26]
- Bethany Hamilton lost her arm in a shark attack at thirteen.[27]
- Barbara Corcoran grew up in poverty with a verbally abusive father, then dropped out of college.[28]
- John Paul DeJoria was raised in foster care and survived an abusive childhood.[29]
- David Geffen grew up with an abusive mother and dropped out of college.[30]
- Richard Pryor grew up in a brothel and endured sexual abuse.[31]
- George Foreman grew up in a tough neighborhood with an abusive stepfather, then dropped out of high school.[32]

---

[24] Ramsay, J. (1995). *Ted Turner: A biography*. HarperCollins.

[25] Lazenby, R. (2014). *Michael Jordan: The life*. Little, Brown.

[26] Smith, J. (2010). *Billionaire cable pioneer: The Alan Gerry story*. Wiley.

[27] Hamilton, B. (2004). *Soul surfer: A true story of faith, family, and fighting to get back on the board*. MTV Books.

[28] Corcoran, B. (2011). *Shark tales: How I turned $1,000 into a billion-dollar business*. Penguin.

[29] DeJoria, J. P. (2018). *Good fortune: How I made it big in business without losing my soul*. Penguin.

[30] Geffen, D. (1997). *The operator: David Geffen builds, buys, and sells the new Hollywood*. Broadway Books.

[31] Pryor, R. (1995). *Pryor convictions: And other life sentences*. Pantheon.

[32] Foreman, G. (2008). *God in my corner: A spiritual memoir*. Thomas Nelson.

- LeBron James was raised by a single mother in poverty.[33]
- Cristiano Ronaldo grew up in poverty on a small Portuguese island.[34]
- Shania Twain grew up in poverty and faced multiple family tragedies.[35]
- Howard Schultz was raised in poverty in Brooklyn.[36]
- Elon Musk was severely bullied as a child and dropped out of Stanford.[37]
- Charlize Theron witnessed her mother killing her abusive father.[38]

Solomon makes it clear: the road to any or all wisdom starts in a single place.

> *The fear of the Lord is the beginning of wisdom, and knowledge of the Holy One is understanding. For through wisdomyour days will be many, and years will be added to your life. (9:10-11).*

You can be as clever as you want; as rich as you can be; or even as ruthless as the worst, but you can never be *wise* if you do

---

[33] Windhorst, B. (2017). *Return of the king: LeBron James, the Cleveland Cavaliers, and the greatest comeback in NBA history.* Grand Central.

[34] Balague, G. (2015). *Cristiano Ronaldo: The biography.* Orion Publishing.

[35] Twain, S. (2011). *From this moment on.* Atria Books.

[36] Schultz, H. (2011). *Onward: How Starbucks fought for its life without losing its soul.* Rodale.

[37] Vance, A. (2015). *Elon Musk: Tesla, SpaceX, and the quest for a fantastic future.* HarperCollins.

[38] Norman, T. (2008). *Charlize Theron: Biography.* Plexus Publishing.

not hold a respectful dread and reverence for God (1:28-29). All wisdom comes from God and belongs to Him (2:6, 8:22-31); it was how He made the world before it existed (3:19-20). Understanding and knowing who He is, as the origin source of wisdom, starts the journey towards it.

Your life will be decided and governed by how you respond to this knowledge (14:12).

If you scoff at it, God says you'll fail if try without Him (14:6, 19:29), avoid wise people (15:12), and be detested by other people (24:9). He mocks you for your pride (3:34). Only severe public punishment will change you (19:25).

If you are lazy, God says your behaviour is ridiculous (22:13) and you'll end up poor (10:4, 20:13) doing work you hate (12:24). He says to study how ants behave (6:6-8).

If you're terminally and pathologically stupid, God makes it clear you are entirely self-deceived (14:8), there is no helping you (14:7) and you'll end up dead because of your own words and deeds (1:32, 8:36, 10:21).

If you're evil and in open rebellion against God, He hates you, curses you, and your home (3:33, 10:29, 15:8-9), rejecting your self-serving cries to Him (21:27). He hates your thoughts (15:26), condemns your schemes (12:2), will expose you (10:9, 26:26) and and will block what you crave (10:3, 22:12).

If you're simple, God says your ways will end in your death (1:32) like a fool's, but you can change if you listen to wise people (21:11) and follow wisdom instead (9:6). You reached a crash point (29:1) because you are gullible (14:15), chased pipedreams (12:11), and were seduced by con-artistry (9:14-18). You loved it (1:22) and it was pleasurable to you (15:21).

God's invitation is to accept correction (19:20) by acknowledging your own ignorance (14:12, 16:25, 21:2, 21:16): start by fearing Him (1:7, 14:16, 22:4, 23:17) and abandoning any association with evil people (1:10-19, 14:16).

Then, answer His call: come to His house and eat (9:4-8). In chapter eight (8: 1-36), he explains why.

How Poor Kids From Nowhere Learn To Speak With Kings

God is a King. He makes kings and rules them (21:1, 29:14). They rule through wisdom, which he created (2:6, 8:22-31), and he gives to them (8:15–16). He teaches people as lowly as you to speak with them (16:13).

Gentlemen aren't born; they are *bred* and *well-read*. Maybe you didn't go to one of those expensive schools and only had the remains of the local library to visit. When educated people talk at dinner parties and embassy dinners, they display their *manners* and distinguish themselves by their reading of *Politics*, *Philosophy*, and *Economics*. You can do that too, without university. Someone taught them, but you can also teach yourself.

Even if you come from nothing, still have nothing, but are able to somehow have access to books on paper or in audio format, time spent reading these could make you the compelling dinner guest of any ambassador. Even with holes in your shoes or in a prison cell.

Gentlemanly Etiquette

Social customs evolve to play an important role in how human beings organise themselves. They are not mere snobbish technicalities. They are how we attempt to emulate Godly characteristics together. Ask yourself, what does this stuffy practice *say* about someone who cares to enough to obey it? What *virtue* does it encourage?

- *The Gentlemen's Book of Etiquette and Manual of Politeness* by Cecil B. Hartley
- *The Ladies' Book of Etiquette, and Manual of Politeness* by Florence Hartley
- *A Complete Hand Book for the Use of the Lady in Polite Society* by Florence Hartley
- *Social Life; or, The Manners and Customs of Polite Society* by Maud C. Cooke
- *Martine's Hand-book of Etiquette, and Guide to True Politeness* by Arthur Martine
- *Principles of Politeness, and of Knowing the World* by Philip Dormer Stanhope, 4th Earl of Chesterfield
- *Beadle's Dime Book of Practical Etiquette for Ladies and Gentlemen* by Anonymous (Published by Beadle and Company)
- *How to Behave: A Pocket Manual of Republican Etiquette, and Guide to Correct Personal Habits* by Samuel R. Wells
- *Debrett's New Guide to Etiquette and Modern Manners: The Indispensable Handbook* by John Morgan
- *How to Behave: A Pocket Manual of Etiquette* by Samuel R. Wells
- *The Honours of the Table, or, Rules for Behaviour During Meals* by Rev. John Trusler

- *A Critical Pronouncing Dictionary* by John Walker
- *American Etiquette and Rules of Politeness* by Walter R. Houghton

The Classics

Work your way through each of these. One to two weeks at a time, as best you can. You don't have to buy them; borrow them from the library or read them free online. Remember key passages, interesting characters, descriptions you liked, and ideas you found curious.

- *The Iliad* by Homer
- *The Odyssey* by Homer
- *The Art of War* by Sun Tzu
- *The Histories* by Herodotus
- *The Peloponnesian War* by Thucydides
- *The Republic* by Plato
- *The Ethics* by Aristotle
- *The Poetics* by Aristotle
- *The Nicomachean Ethics* by Aristotle
- *The Aeneid* by Virgil
- *Meditations* by Marcus Aurelius
- *The Analects* by Confucius
- *The Histories* by Tacitus
- *The Confessions* by Augustine of Hippo
- *The Divine Comedy* by Dante Alighieri
- *The Decameron* by Giovanni Boccaccio
- *The Canterbury Tales* by Geoffrey Chaucer
- *The Prince* by Niccolò Machiavelli
- *Utopia* by Thomas More

- *The Essays* by Michel de Montaigne
- *Don Quixote* by Miguel de Cervantes
- *Hamlet* by William Shakespeare
- *King Lear* by William Shakespeare
- *Paradise Lost* by John Milton
- *Leviathan* by Thomas Hobbes
- *An Essay Concerning Human Understanding* by John Locke
- *Two Treatises of Government* by John Locke
- *Candide* by Voltaire
- *The Social Contract* by Jean-Jacques Rousseau
- *A Treatise of Human Nature* by David Hume
- *An Enquiry Concerning Human Understanding* by David Hume
- *The Sorrows of Young Werther* by Johann Wolfgang von Goethe
- *The Wealth of Nations* by Adam Smith
- *The Theory of Moral Sentiments* by Adam Smith
- *Principles of Political Economy and Taxation* by David Ricardo
- *Reflections on the Revolution in France* by Edmund Burke
- *Principles of Political Economy* by John Stuart Mill
- *The Federalist Papers* by Alexander Hamilton, James Madison, and John Jay
- *Critique of Pure Reason* by Immanuel Kant
- *Pride and Prejudice* by Jane Austen
- *Frankenstein* by Mary Shelley
- *Democracy in America* by Alexis de Tocqueville
- *Wuthering Heights* by Emily Brontë
- *Jane Eyre* by Charlotte Brontë
- *Madame Bovary* by Gustave Flaubert
- *Les Misérables* by Victor Hugo

- *The Scarlet Letter* by Nathaniel Hawthorne
- *Moby-Dick* by Herman Melville
- *On Liberty* by John Stuart Mill
- *The Adventures of Huckleberry Finn* by Mark Twain
- *Crime and Punishment* by Fyodor Dostoevsky
- *On the Origin of Species* by Charles Darwin
- *War and Peace* by Leo Tolstoy
- *Anna Karenina* by Leo Tolstoy
- *The Brothers Karamazov* by Fyodor Dostoevsky
- *Thus Spoke Zarathustra* by Friedrich Nietzsche
- *Middlemarch* by George Eliot
- *The Picture of Dorian Gray* by Oscar Wilde
- *The Interpretation of Dreams* by Sigmund Freud
- *The Metamorphosis* by Franz Kafka
- *In Search of Lost Time* by Marcel Proust
- *Ulysses* by James Joyce
- *To the Lighthouse* by Virginia Woolf
- *The Great Gatsby* by F. Scott Fitzgerald
- *The Waste Land* by T.S. Eliot
- *Four Quartets* by T.S. Eliot
- *The Stranger* by Albert Camus
- *Mere Christianity* by C.S. Lewis
- *The Abolition of Man* by C.S. Lewis
- *The Catcher in the Rye* by J.D. Salinger
- *Nineteen Eighty-Four* by George Orwell
- *Brave New World* by Aldous Huxley
- *The Road to Serfdom* by Friedrich Hayek
- *The Constitution Of Liberty* by Friedrich Hayek
- *One Hundred Years of Solitude* by Gabriel García Márquez
- *To Kill a Mockingbird* by Harper Lee

When You Attend The Embassy

With enough reading, the day will come. When it does, fitted clothes are better than fashionable. Classic, conservative elegance beats extravagance; modesty and humility beat prosperity; honest trumps impressive. Less is always more.

- Pray for the right words (16:1).
- Bring a small, thoughtful unique gift (18:16).
- Wait to be invited or called for (25:6-7).
- Be extremely careful of how you speak (17:7).
- You're being observed (23:1-3).
- Listen first (18:13).
- Speak gracefully (25:15) with wise timing (10:32).
- Avoid alcohol (20:1).
- Don't boast or over-share (12:23).
- Don't gossip (11:13) or flatter (29:5-6)
- Do not linger over beautiful attendees (5:8, 7:25).
- Praise people with good motives (22:11).
- Speak gently of the poor (18:23).
- Never praise yourself (27:2).
- Eat beforehand. Then eat lightly and sparingly (23: 1-3).
- Be a pleasant conversationalist (15:23).
- Remember a King's life is burden (16:15) and dealing with opportunists (11:6).
- Kings are fathers with children (19:14).
- Don't fake it to make it (12:9, 13:7).
- Avoid any conflicts or rivalries (26:17).
- Duplicity or intrigue will bring you ruin (11:3).
- Speak humbly of your desire for excellence (22:29).
- Don't speak of any association with troublemakers or

revolutionaries (24:21-22).
- Never criticise a loyal employee (30:10) and protect your boss (27:18).
- Be patient and overlook offence (19:11).
- Help to calm those in authority (16:14).
- Recognition of your intelligence and prudence will bring you honour (12:8).
- Recognition of your proven, good, and wise judgment will bring you favour (13:15).
- Reputation is more important than wealth (22:1).

The eloquent words of John Adams on May 26, 1785, as he stood after a bloody civil war in front of what was the most powerful man in the world, exemplify the wisdom of 25:11:

"Sir, The United States of America have appointed me their Minister Plenipotentiary to your Majesty . . . It is in Obedience to their express Commands that I have the Honor to assure your Majesty of their unanimous Disposition and Desire to cultivate the most friendly and liberal Intercourse between your Majesty's Subjects and their Citizens . . . The appointment of a Minister from the United States to your Majesty's Court, will form an Epocha in the History of England & of America. I think myself more fortunate than all my fellow Citizens in having the distinguished Honor to be the first to stand in your Majesty's royal Presence in a diplomatic Character; and I shall esteem myself the happiest of men if I can be instrumental in recommending my country more and more to your Majesty's royal benevolence, and of restoring an entire esteem, confidence, and affection, or,

in better words, the old good nature and the old good humor between people, who, though separated by an ocean and under different governments, have the same language, a similar religion, and kindred blood. I beg your Majesty's permission to add that although I have some time before been instructed by my country, it was never in my whole life in a manner so agreeable to myself."

To which King George replied,

"The circumstances of this audience are so extraordinary, the language you have now held is so extremely proper, and the feelings you have discovered so justly adapted to the occasion, that I must say that I not only receive with pleasure the assurance of the friendly dispositions of the United States, but that I am very glad that the choice has fallen upon you to be the minister. I wish you, sir, to believe, and that it be understood in America, that I have done nothing in the late contest but what I thought myself indispensably bound to do by the duty which I owed to my people. I will be very frank with you, I was the last to consent to separation; but the separation having been made, and having become inevitable, I have always said, as I say now, that I would be the first to meet the friendship of the United States as an independent power. Let the Circumstances of Language; Religion and Blood have their natural and full Effect."